I0833241

Ernesto Vega Jánica
Hugues Vega Murgas
Simón Esmeral Ariza

Cover by
Connie Gómez

The book **Pueblo Iku: Science, Nature and Art of the Arhuaco** analyzes our most recent studies and learning experiences related to this pre-Hispanic indigenous community that still exists today in the northern region of Colombia, South America. This document is a simple attempt to raise awareness of the magnificent skills in STEM (Science, Technology, Engineering and Mathematics) of the Iku or Arhuaco people, and how they have preserved their knowledge and applied science in harmony with nature and other civilizations.

Authors. **Ernesto Vega Jánica, Hugues Vega Murgas y Simón Esmeral Ariza**

Editor. **Ernesto Vega Jánica**

Recognized as the 2017 Fire Protection Engineer of the Year by the Society of Fire Protection Engineers (SFPE), New Jersey Chapter, United States; and awarded the 2011 Tyco Patent Award as author of a patent application on fire alarm visual notification appliances, Mr. Vega Janica is the author of multiple technical documents and international presentations in the field of engineering and application of optimization models. Mr. Vega Jánica, a graduate alumni of the University of Maryland, U.S., is also a math enthusiast and his research on multiple numerical systems has taken him to humanitarian work and STEM (Science, Technology, Engineering and Mathematics). Mr. Vega Jánica is also an instructor of international technical standards and the author or Native Mathematics 5, a children textbook focus on Indigenous Math methods and their integration to current educational curriculums.

ISBN-13: 978-0-9997757-3-8

U.S. Copyright Office. Registration Number TXu 2-179-650

First edition: November 11, 2020

Introduction…

Pueblo Ikʉ: Ciencia, Naturaleza y Arte Arhuaco

La opción perfecta tanto para educadores y padres, como para historiadores y amantes de las lenguas y culturas nativas. Este valioso texto combina aspectos socio culturales, reseñas históricas e invaluables conceptos de la vida cotidiana y creencias de nuestros pueblos Arhuacos (o Ikʉ). El libro incluye un sinnúmero de imágenes, mapas, tablas y diagramas con información relevante para la conservación de la naturaleza y cultura indígena. Además, este libro incluye ejercicios prácticos y actividades emocionantes, en un entorno actual y con ámbito global. Las páginas reproducibles brindan a los estudiantes la práctica que necesitan para dominar las habilidades básicas necesarias, y son excelentes para usar tanto en la escuela como en el hogar.

Habilidades incluidas:

- Etno-Educación enfocada a la cultura Arhuaca
- Orígenes Mitológicos
- Lenguaje
- Localización
- Costumbres y Tradiciones
- Materia, Energía y el Universo Ikʉ
- Fauna y Flora Ikʉ
- El Suelo y Las Piedras
- El Aire y El Agua
- Números Ikʉ y Otros Sistemas Numéricos Indígenas
- Actividades Pedagógicas

Dedicado a las culturas nativas del nuevo continente, a su historia, su sabiduría y sus enseñanzas para futuras generaciones.

Completamente Bilingüe:
Español-Lengua Ikʉn

How to navigate thru this book...

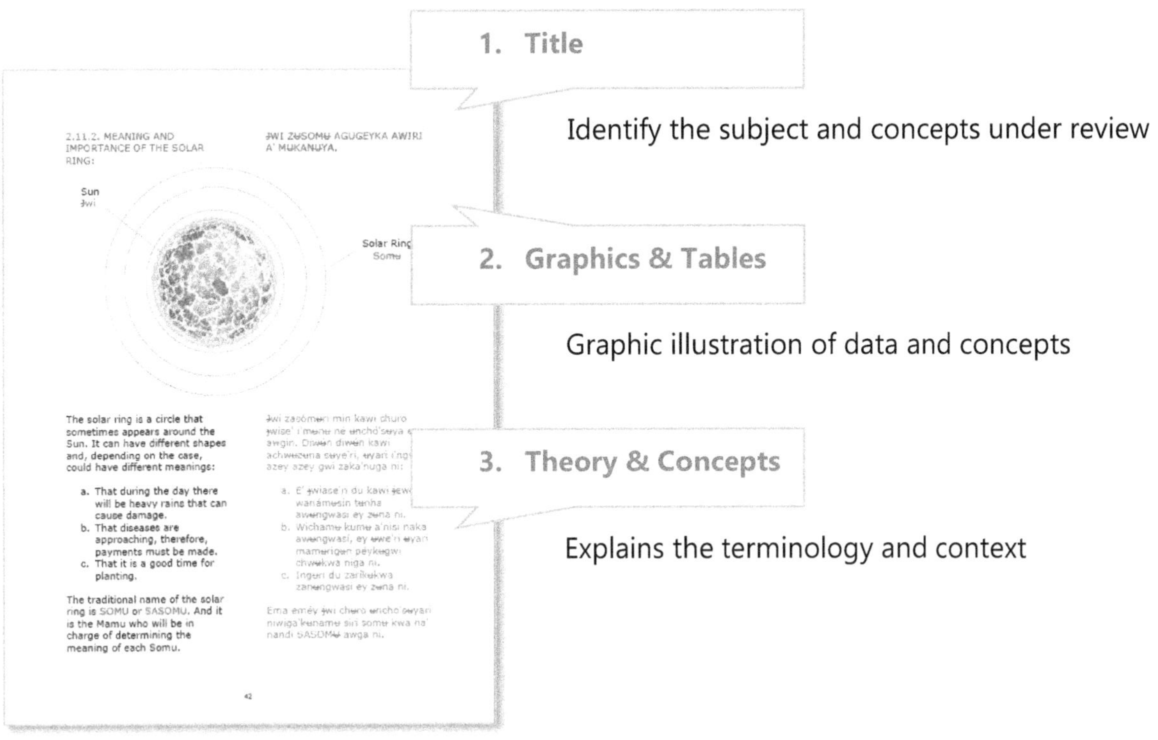

Identify the subject and concepts under review

Graphic illustration of data and concepts

Explains the terminology and context

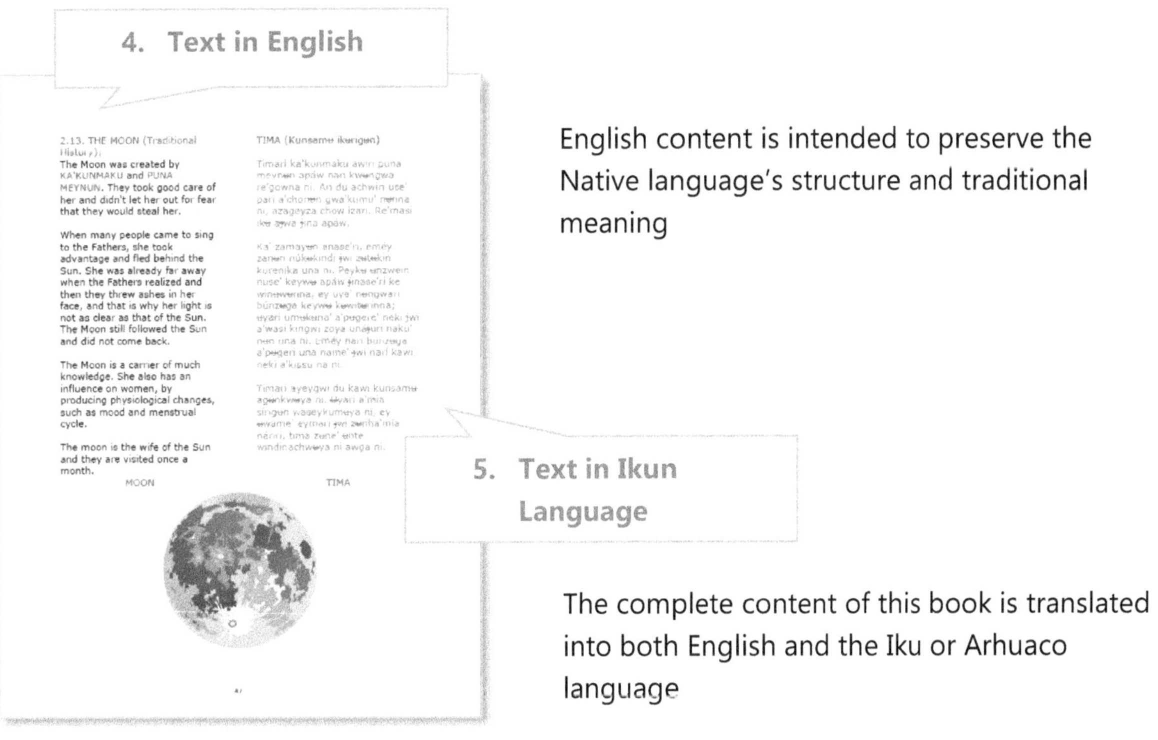

English content is intended to preserve the Native language's structure and traditional meaning

The complete content of this book is translated into both English and the Iku or Arhuaco language

6. Games & Activities

Games and other pedagogical activities in which we can put into practice the lessons learned on each Chapter

4.5. PEDAGOGICAL ACTIVITIES:
Classify animals according to their habitat.

NIKAMʉ
Emi ana'nuga chwʉzʉneykari azey azey kwʉyeyka chwʉzʉnhasa awkwa.

7. Indigenous Math

Basic concepts and exercises using multiple numerical systems, and tools, developed by many native Latin American civilizations

In that vast geographical area, the pre-Columbian civilizations of the Incas, Aztecs and Maya flourished until their annihilation during the Spanish conquest in the fifteenth and sixteenth centuries (1400-1600).

The brutality of the conquest along with some inter-tribal wars fragmented these great civilizations, leaving only scattered descendants with little cultural connection with their ancestors.

However, the advanced numerical systems of these societies have survived and could

Eymanke' ka'gumʉ awʉtari zari nʉna'ba, Incas, Azteca, awin Maya eygumʉn awʉtari inʉ chuzʉnhasi rizwein nu'nari sémʉke bunachʉ España zanʉ neykase' winde'rijo'si siglo XV awiri XVI (1400-1600) ey awkin chʉká a'zʉnnari, yow izátikumʉkin.

Ema ka'gumʉ ke awari zoya gugin arunhu nari ey awi keywʉri agʉnke' a'kwey rizoya jinari ʉnwinʉnkʉripanʉn pana ʉweykasindi ema jinari yow winʉkʉnichona una ni, in'gwi atʉgʉnkekʉ winkwey zoya jina zʉn chúkumey. Emey ʉwe'ki, izʉnchʉnhakumʉya neykari eyki

143

Table of Content

Table of Content

Table of Content

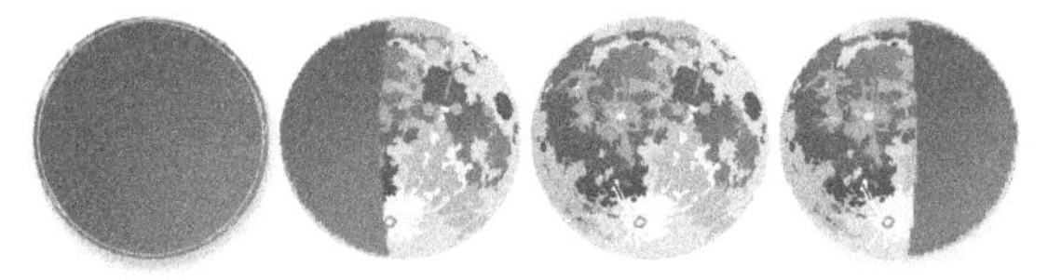

Table of Content

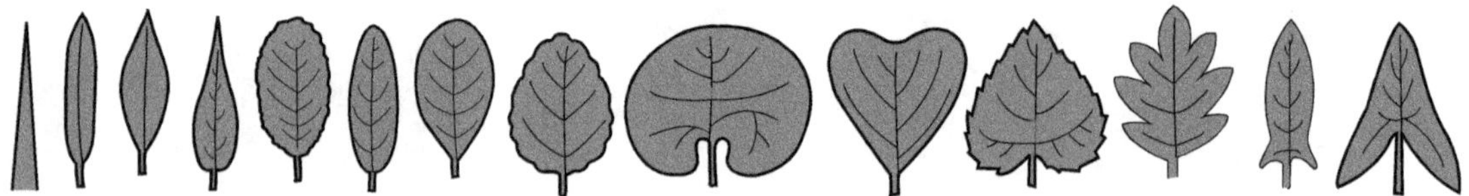

Table of Content

Table of Content

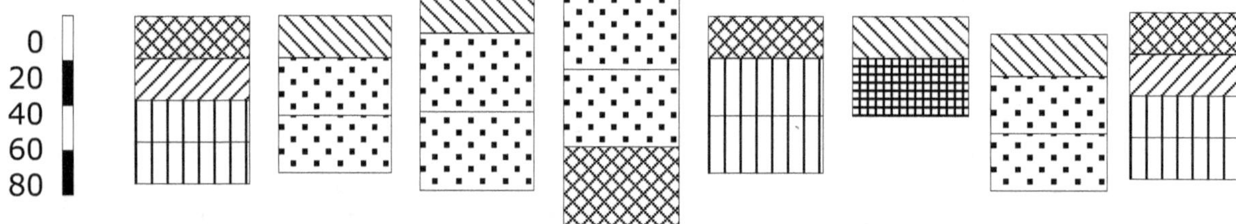

Table of Content

Table of Content

Table of Content

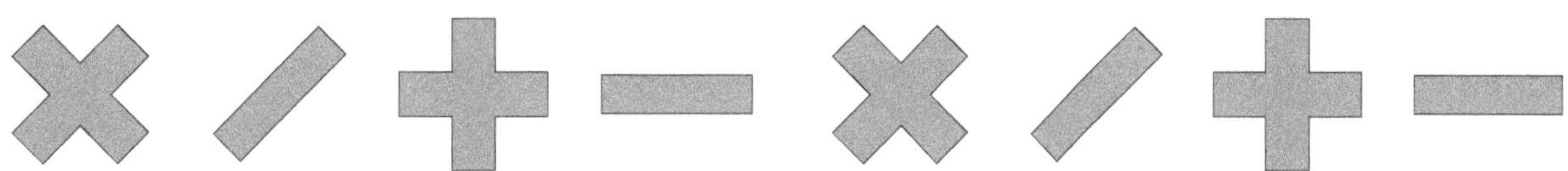

Introduction

The cultural wisdom of the Arhuaco people and other indigenous communities must be of great pride for our current and future generations. The study and documentation of their knowledge are a tool to better understand our relationship with the world around us and our role in nature, science and art.

Furthermore in this book, we will see some practical and didactic elements that we hope will bring our children closer to learning, respect and love this community of the Iku, also known as the Arhuacos.

The initial conception of this book is based on our research related to multiple numerical systems used by various indigenous communities, as well as other tools of science, technology, engineering and mathematics (STEM), which, although much more specific to a single civilization; It could be a great example for many people and future generations. Our intent is to provide a social and humanitarian service by preserving part of this culture and language that we still have the privilege of knowing.

We hope, then, the concepts in this book will be of great value to you and your families.

Chuzʉnhakumey zoyana wásʉya

Ema arwaku neyka awiri in'geygwi ikʉ nenanki ikʉnha nari winʉwa'ba dukawa winʉkʉnari aweykari eygwi wininayʉn nugga awiri eygwi winkwakumʉngwa ɉina neykazeyri zeyzey wina'chwi winchwiza nanunanno. Kʉrigawi uneyka awiri paperi bori uneyka inʉ zana pinnase' ka'mʉkanagwi awikeywʉri kʉrigawía unige'ri zaku ɉina nanʉn nugeykari ʉyasingwi ʉnkʉnʉnkura na'nó niwe'zʉn awiri chow a'chwa awniwingwa nari nanu nanno.

Eymi pariri, in'gwi ɉuná neyka kʉrigawiwkwey kawi kʉrigata'na neykari gʉmʉsinʉse'ri wina'riguzari, chow a'chwi nʉnnige'ri arwaku aneykase'ri peykʉ twiré yʉngwa nanu nanno.

Sekʉnari kʉrigawí ʉweyka ikʉ inʉ winʉkizʉnchʉnhey uweyka awi pinna ɉunakʉchʉ sekʉnari ukumaneykase' anipʉnsiri ema kʉriwiwkweyna a'chunhakumʉngwa ni'na ni, eygumʉn in'gwi kinki nʉnnandi eygumʉ dukawi renari zʉnnanki awanʉnki ema neykari ingweti akwey azoyanke neki a'mʉkanagwi awiza na'nanno awanʉn nusi emari nanu nanno; ey awkweygwi niwikʉnʉna'bari.

Ey awʉndi, emi a'nikwʉyari awʉtari a'zʉna miwikʉnika miwi awiri in'gwi re'kwa nenanki eyma iawa'kʉngwa ni.

ARHUACOS OR IKʉ INDIGENOUS PEOPLE

1. ORIGEN

According to the mythological believes of the Arhuacos, before the materialization of the living beings in nature, everything was darkness and that everything comes from Mother Earth, Séynekun[1], and Father Sun, Bunkwakukwi[2].

For the Iku, the four fundamental elements of nature are water, earth, air and fire.

The Arhuaco people are made up of four castes.

A'BUNNA

Kunsamʉ wina'rigʉnkuya ikʉ na'ba winyeykari, emi pinna chʉká a'zari chuzari ʉweyka eykigwi zaniku'gwi nʉnkwe'ri, yowkʉchʉ seyhʉn (twi zari) zʉn zʉnna ni awiri zaku ka'gʉmʉ Seynekʉn awiri kakʉ Bunkwakukwi na'ba gunti keywʉ zanikʉn pʉnna ni.

Ikʉ neykase'ri, ma'keywa ʝuna neyka awʉtari a'zʉneyka winʉwánʉyari ema ni: ʝe, ka', wamʉ awiri gey.

Ikʉ winneyka ʝinari ma'keywa re'kwa winneyka ni.

[1] Name of Mother Earth

[2] Name of Father Sun

Together they are currently more than 45,000 individuals.

In recent years, they have managed to form Cabildos Gobernadores[3] that have proved to be an adequate form of organization to defend their indigenous values and territories.

1.1. CASTES

Men	Women
Busintana	Gwewkwa
Serankuatana	Gumuku
Geyninkekatana	Chacaimeina
Gunkuto	Gumuke

1.2. LANGUAGE

Their language comes from the Chibcha linguistic family, which uses a subject-object-verb sentence structure.

For example:
"I like to learn from Nature and Animals"

1.3. LOCATION

Located in the Sierra Nevada de Santa Marta in northern Colombia. The Arhuacos consider the Sierra Nevada and its peaks at more than 5,700 m (18,700 ft), as the heart of our planet. Its surroundings form a complex system that helps maintain balance with our ecosystem.

Yowkʉchʉ 45000 kawʉwinde'rinikuya ni.

Kʉggi mʉcheygʉmʉri, kawirdu Gobernador, kʉnari awʉngweyka winde'rigukaki nugga ni, ema neykari du kawi winde'rigusi awi keywʉri ema ikʉ na'ba winʉnkwey ka'gʉmʉ ikwey awiri kunsamʉ.

TANA

CHEYRWA	A'MÍA
Busintana tana	Gwewkwa tana
Serankwa tana	Gumʉku tana
Geyningeka tana	Chʉkay tana
Gúnkʉtʉ tana	Gumʉke tana

WINÁSʉYA

Winasʉyari in'gweygwi tana ikʉgwi neyka CHIBCHA za'kinu'nase' zanʉ winasy nanno; azi name' awanʉndi ga'gónuga ya'bari waseykumʉya, ínʉki, waníkʉnʉ.

Ema zanʉzana:
Ana'nuga awiri pinna chuzari ʉwa neyka kʉriwiwna'ɉúya ni.

WINKUYA'BA

Niwiúmʉke Colombia za'kinuga azwʉrʉnkiay úmʉnʉkʉnʉ sierra nevada aya'ba winkuya ni. Ikʉ arhuaku neykase'ri kwímʉkʉnʉ nusi ɉʉn iyunusi zanʉn nugeykari ema ka'gʉmʉ aɉu zʉɉwawika winʉnka'chwʉya ni. Ana'nuga, ɉe, kʉnkʉnʉ, kwímʉkʉnʉ, zari zoyaki

[3] Civil Authority of the Territory/Indigenous Reservation

The Arhuacos, or Pueblo Iku, are descendants of the Tayronas, an indigenous tribe that inhabited the Don Diego, Palomino, Buritaca and Guachaca rivers, in the Sierra Nevada de Santa Marta.

nugga dikin a'kusʉn nugga awari warunhʉya ni.

Ikʉ arhuaku winneykari Tayrona tana winneykani, ikʉ tana Don Diego meyna, Palominu meyna, Buritaka awiri Gwachaka ɟe swí yuri ʉwa meyna winkwana nanu nanno.

In the following textbooks:
Magdalena mi Departamento,

Cesar mi Departamento,
ISBN: 978-958-44-8313-3

La Guajira mi Departamento,
ISBN: 978-958-33-7511-X

Colombia mi Patria,
ISBN: 978-958-44-8314-0

More details can be found on socio-cultural, economic, historical and even flora and fauna aspects of the Departments of Cesar, Magdalena and La Guajira, as well as about all of Colombia.

These are, therefore, recommended readings for students, educators and parents.

Ema neykari emi mika'chónukwa ni.
Magdalena mi Departamento,

Cesar mi Departamento,
ISBN: 978-958-44-8313-3

La Guajira mi Departamento,
ISBN: 978-958-33-7511-X

Colombia mi Patria,
ISBN: 978-958-44-8314-0

Eymi na'ba ema kwey winzoya'ba wásʉya, ɉwisin winagawi zoya'ba wásʉya, mʉnágwi a'zari arunhey winnakʉn nuggan wásʉya, kwa kʉn ɉuna sírigʉn, aná'nuga sí neki, migʉnchona ɉunʉndi yʉkweyna emey za'kinugase' a'nikwʉya ni.

Ema neykagun, yʉkweynari paperi ya ɉúnʉyase' agawiwyʉn, ʉnkʉriwiwyase' awiri gʉmʉsinʉ zʉpaw winnanʉn nugeykase'.

Let's teach and learn from each other. We are brothers and sisters to one another.

1.4 CUSTOMES AND TRADITIONS

1.4.1. KNITTING AND WEAVING

Knitting is a traditional work that women do, although men knit their blankets and hats.

It is a work that they combine with all daily activities, especially when they walk on the roads, in their spare time, and so on. Girls weave even at school recesses.

Blankets and mochilas (napshacks) are waved with sheep wool and cotton they spin and manufacture on their own.

In some cases, fique is also used to make mochilas.

Women prepare cotton and sheep wool yarn so that men can make their blankets, hats and sandals.

AYEY DUWINA'Z\u0289NEYKA AWIRI KUNSAM\u0289

IN\u0289 WIN\u0289NKISI ZOYEYKA

Tutu isi awkweykari nikam\u0289 kunsám\u0289se' k\u0289n\u0289na a'míazey nari kinki nanu nanno, cheyrwa \u0268inari ayeygwi tutusoma win\u0289nkisagwi awiri m\u0289k\u0289 win\u0289ngowgwi aw\u0289nki.
Nikam\u0289 siggin, ayey du k\u0289re'kusana nanu nanno ingeygwi awkwa nekaw\u0289nki, beki zwein nugge, ing\u0289 m\u0289n\u0289kin k\u0289zana tán\u0289ye', kwa eygum\u0289n neki.

G\u0289m\u0289sin\u0289 a'miágum\u0289 neki arekwera nugga m\u0289n\u0289kin k\u0289zana tán\u0289ye' ayeygwi is\u0289ya ni.
M\u0289k\u0289 awiri tutu neykari weja awiri unk\u0289 neykasin winaw\u0289ya ní.

Bech\u0289 ayeygwi tutu winis\u0289ya'bagwi am\u0289k\u0289nhas\u0289ya ni.

A'mía \u0268ina neykari unk\u0289 awiri weja winbúns\u0289ya ni, emari neykari cheyrwa m\u0289k\u0289 awiri tutusoma win\u0289nkisi aw\u0289ngwasi awiri s\u0289patu sin\u0289 \u0289nka'cho's\u0289ngwasi.

1.4.2. TYPICAL DRESS

In the Arhuaco ethnic group, both men and women use a completely white dress or white blanket with stripes, made by themselves.

Now days, some individuals buy these fabrics in warehouses in neighboring towns and cities.

Men wear a complete white hat that symbolizes the snow at the peak of the Sierra Nevada, and together with their long hair represents the mountains and trees around their territory; That is why it is forbidden for them to cut their hair.

Men start wearing the hat from the age of 14 or 15.

MɄKɄ WINAJɄYEYKA

Ikʉ arwaku winnʉna'bari, cheyrwa kwa a'mía ne gwa' awʉnki mʉkʉ winajʉya'bari bunsi kawi zʉn neyka ni, kwa bunsi kawi kigesi kwa ka'gesi nʉngwi ʉwa ni, ikʉnha winʉnkowna.

In'gwiri bunachʉkeyna ʉnwinʉnkisari awagwi ʉwa ni.

Cheyrwa ɉina neykari tutusoma winanisi neykani, eymari kunsamʉ rigʉndi ɉʉn kʉzʉna neyka ni awiri ságʉnʉ neykari gari kawi neykari kʉ́nkʉnʉ awiri kwímʉkʉnʉ kʉzʉna ni winguga ni; emey ʉwame' ʉnbey awkwa winʉka'nikwʉya nuki nanu neyka ni.

Cheyrwa neyka tutusomari in'gwi uga ma'keywa kwa asewa kʉttow kʉggi izánige' winde'sʉya ni.

1.5. HANDCRAFTS

The handmade pieces they make are mainly for personal, work and commercial use.

For example,
The baskets are used to collect coffee, load Jayo leaves (Coca leaves), saved sheep wool, etc.

Mochilas are an indispensable element in their daily life.

They also use mortars to grind corn, which is the basis of their diet.

The most used musical instruments are drums, reeds and accordion.

GÚNʉKʉNʉ

Pinna gúnʉsin inʉ winʉnkawi rizoyeykari ikʉnha kingwi winʉnka'rika'mʉnhasʉngwa neyka ni, nikámʉzey nari awiri winʉnkʉngeykʉngwa nʉngwi ʉwa ni.

Eyma zanʉzanari, katáwiri neki gow ʉwe'ri eymari café ʉnkʉtakʉngwa, ayu takʉngwa, weja du ʉnkawʉngwa awiri eygumʉnkʉchʉ.

Tutu neykari siginkʉchʉ inʉ owkumey zoya'ba kʉjunʉya ni.

Ayeygwi pironʉsingwi in winʉnkichusʉya ni zamʉ winʉnkʉre'ritasi ʉwa'ba.

A'kari ɉina winʉkʉnari ʉwaneykari kaja, charu kordion neyka ni.

1.6. DANCES

The Arhuacos perform dances for fun in family gatherings, and also for the reactivation of positive energies with nature.

For example,
They dance in birthdays and marriages, baptisms, in the inauguration of new houses, and for the benefit and blessing of food and crops; and in some cases, they dance so that the rain does not harm their crops, and that the crops remain free of pests.

WINA'RIKWEWYA

arwaku neykari inʉ a'kweamʉ neykasin zeyzey winde'rikusʉya ni, ʉnkʉn ni'kumʉyʉn, in'gwi re'kwa winnʉna'ba awiri ánugwe duna neyka zaku ɉina neyka izeywámʉsi.

Eyma zanʉzana neykari, kwakumanin izeywámʉsi, ɉwa ʉnbónʉyʉn, ɉwa ʉnkʉkúmʉyʉn, urakʉ abiti agázʉyʉn awiri zamʉ ɉuna awiri chey neykazey nari; e'mʉnʉ́ri ɉewʉ wa'mʉsu' nanʉngwasi awiri cheyri chun dunanu neykase' wa'mʉ isu nanʉngwasi eney nisi rizoya ni.

1.7. THE POPORO

The Porporo is the mythical representation of man and woman. The pumpkin shell represents the woman and the stick inside is the man.

It is used only by men.

Poporo supplements are Jayo and lime. The powder it contains is based on processed sea shells.

Ambil[4], which is a plant of the tobacco family, and that produces a very particular honey, is mixed with Jayo and is used to protect from animal stings.

The Arhuacos use the poporo in moments of concentration, reflection and in the confirmation of greeting each other, in which they exchange Jayo or coca leaves that they carry in their mochilas.

The Jayo is very important for the Arhuacos, since they use it as a key to open ancestral doors and communicate with the mythical beings and with their Gods.

ɈO'BURU

Eyma neykari kunsamʉrigʉndi cheyrwa awiri a'mía zana neyka naní. Sori a'mía nari iwa kʉn so'kʉnʉri cheyrwa nari.

Emari cheyrwa neykase' nʉkin zʉn ʉwa ni.

Ɉo'búruse' kʉnari zoyari ayu awiri ɉo'tinpʉsi neyka ni. Inpʉsiri ɉo'tinwʉ ʉnkʉsinhakumana neyka ni.

Ɉwa awgari, kʉn ɉuna tawaku awga tana neyka ni, eymari ayey awi bostesanari gunti mieri re'bónʉya ni, eymari áyuse' ibiriri ukumʉya ni awiri eymari mika'sá nanʉndi ana'nuga migʉkweyna mʉchey mikʉniku nánʉkwa ni.

Ikʉ arwaku awgari ɉo'búruri awʉtari arunhkwa kawa'ba' rigʉnchónukwa kawa'ba zʉn áwʉya ni, winde'rimásʉya kawari ayu winʉnkʉnta'sa re'pasi eymari gʉgʉwinde'tósʉya kawa neyka ni, ziɉuse' ayu ka'pʉnkwanasin.

Ayu neykari awʉtari a'zʉna neyka ni, eymasin keywʉ ánugwe rigʉndi yawi zana' nari zaku ánugwe nari w'akʉn nugárigʉn o'kʉtʉ kumʉsénʉya ni.

[4] Creole Tobacco Paste

1.8. THE MAMOS

The Manos are a source to knowledge and serve as interpreters of nature and the universe.

They are advisors, harmonizers and maintain the balance between nature and man.

They are at the service of society and act as doctors and priests.

For example,
Moms do an analysis to the child when giving birth, to determine his chances of being a Mamo; If the child is born with the umbilical cord wrapped in the neck or arm, it is the first sign that he can be.

The Mamo always dresses completely in white blanket or white blanket with stripes.

MAMʉ ɈINA

Mamʉ neykari kunsamʉ kwey zoya'ba kawanikwʉya neykan ni awiri ema zaku ásʉyeyka re'zágisʉn nugga neyka ni.

Gwamʉ yeyka zʉn neyka ni, tanʉzakusʉya zʉn neyka ni, awiri ikʉ awiri zaku ɉinasin dikin riwanʉn migwa'sʉkwa neyka ni. Re'masi neykazey nari neyka ni awiri wichamʉ chwagwi awiri pari zana' neyka ni.

Eyma zanʉzana:
Mamʉ ɉinari ema winchwʉya ni, zizi neki akʉnkawʉ neki ga'na a'mʉ́ kwa gákʉna neki imʉ́ nari kwakumʉndi eymari MAMɄ nisiza ni gwasiri Mamʉ nanʉngwa re'bónuya ni.

MAMɄ neykari mʉkʉ bunsi kawi kinki zʉn ʉnkʉcho'sʉya ni. In'gwise'ri ka'gesi nʉngwi ʉwani.

1.9. ADMINISTRATIVE ORGANIZATION

The first place within the administrative organization of the Arhuacos is occupied by the Mamos.

Then, there is the Central Directive that includes four members of the community that fulfill the following functions: governor, prosecutor, treasurer and secretary.

The General Assembly is next, and it is where the leaders of the forty settlements of the Sierra Nevada de Santa Marta participate.

1.9.1. THE HIGHEST AUTHORITY

The Sakuku is the traditional Authority of the community, a person who is guiding and defending the interests of the Iku people in all their trajectories and struggles.

INʉ WINʉNKʉCHWI AWIZʉNA'BA WINDE'RIGU'NA

Inʉ winʉnkʉchwi awiza na'bari arwaku nʉnanke'ri MAMʉ keywʉ neyka ni.

Ey unayu nʉngwari DIREKTIWU ɟina keywʉ nanu nanno, eymari ma'keywa winnneykani, awiri diwʉn diwʉn nikamʉ winkʉnʉna, eymari: kawirdu Gowernador, fiscal, tesorero awiri secretario.

Eymi pariri, ASAMBLEA awga keywʉ nanu nanno, eymari sakuku ɟina zʉnekʉ powru zʉnay winʉnni'kumey zoya ey agwaku nanno.

1.9.1 SAKUKU ACHʉNA

Sakuku achʉna awgari, mʉná powru ka'mʉkari, gunamʉ re'masi gunamʉ agisi zweín nugga ey awga ni. Pinna tanʉ a'zariza nanʉndi a'zari.

1.9.2. AMBASSADOR ARHUACO

It is a position that has the same characteristics of an ambassador or the chancellor of the Colombian government. It is performed by an Arhuaco, who at international and national level seeks social support, recognition and respect for native people.

He is in charge of managing projects that benefit his ethnic group and tries to recover the lands that have been expropriated and that belong to them from their ancestors.

ARWAKU EMBAJADOR

Emari ikʉ ne'ki Embajador kwa canciller awga Gowiernuse' kʉnʉna neykasin akingwi nikamʉ kʉnʉna ey awgani. Ema nikamʉri ikʉse' kʉnari zʉnekʉ nay rigʉnsi ɟwi tasi neyka ey awga ni.

Eme neykari proyectu neki kʉremi'ri awiri ka'gʉmʉ neki asari awiza si neki asay nʉya ey awga na'nanno.

1.10. LEGEND OF THE ARHUACA BACKPACK (MOCHILA ARHUACA)

According to legend, Atynawowa (Sacred Lagoon in the Highlands of the Sierra Nevada, and Mother of the Mochilas) received from Mother Nature the knowledge to weave mochilas, but She behaved in an unconscious and promiscuous way. Then, when her son grew up, he punished her to wave mochilas and to represent throughout various designs, the different moral laws that women should know, respect and fulfill.

A mochila is given to each woman at baptism, and it means that "without her mochila, woman would have no wisdom" and that "by weaving a mochila, she learns cultural values". Waving a mochila takes between 6 to 10 weeks.

Men do not make mochilas.

Usually, Arhuacos carry three mochilas: one for the poporo and the greeting Ayo; a second one is used to bring gifts; and the third one is the most important one, mainly because it is where the elements of personal use are carried. The third mochila serves as a purse or bag for western women and as an executive briefcase for men.

KUNSAMʉ TUTU ÍKʉZEY WASEYKUMʉYA.

Kunsámʉse' waseykumʉyari, (Atinawowa tutu zaku) emase' keywʉ tutu isamʉ neykari a'gowna ni, ey ukwe'ki du neki nanu nari du niku nari in'gwi in'gwi cheyrwa a'zari zoyanari gunti gʉmʉsinʉ gosa zoyana. Gʉmʉsinʉ kinaya ukwe'ri zi a'zey awiri, ey anʉweykasdin, ari pinna ɉuna tutu cho'samʉ anʉkʉriwiana, arunhey awkweyka, a'mía neyka ema awi zwein pana única ge'; awiri ema neykari ayey wazweingwa nari.

Tutu neykari ingweti wekumana neyka ni, a'mía neyka tutu isu nanʉndi emari arunhey awkweykari kinay nari zorizani, emasindi pinna chow a'chwamʉ riwingwasi neyka ni. In'gweti nʉnay chinwa kwa in'gwi uga semana zʉne kʉwisi zoya ni. Cheyrwa achʉna neykari tutu isu neyka ni.

Arwaku neykari máykʉnʉ tutu neki a'cheygékuya ni: in'gwir ayu mʉssi, eymasindi ayu re'pasʉngwa, in'gwiri ínʉki neki re'kawʉngwa rekʉsʉngwa kwa agakównige' neki rekʉsʉngwa. Ema neykari e'mʉnʉ ne'ri mʉkʉ neki rekʉpasi nayʉngwa nʉngwi ʉwa ni.

1.11. NABUSIMAKE

NABUSIMAKE

Nabusimake is the capital of the majestic and mythical Arhuaco universe. At first it was called Busímake, which means "Earth where the Sun is born".

Nestled in a plain at 2,700 meters (8,800 ft) above sea level, bathed by rivers and streams, it is an enigmatic, fertile and beautiful place that could well be called the paradise of Department of Cesar, where the waterfall or waterfall of the Kurakatá and the Devil and the Tetas spa wells are located.

The "Pueblito Arhuaco" as it is affectionately called, is the meeting place of the forty indigenous settlements that

Ema neykari aúmʉ neykani, ema poeru arwaku neykazey nari. Kʉtʉnʉn keywʉri BISÍMʉKE za'kinu'na ni, "ka'gʉmʉse' kakʉ Bunkwakukwi kwákumanin"

Ema neykari 2.700 metru nánʉkin warin zari nanʉn nugga ni, aya'bari, ɉe swí kʉnʉngwi, awʉ'te kawa kʉnʉngwi, awi gunti du zʉn zʉna ni, aganke'ri pinzʉnay ɉe uzweí nigga nani, eyma neykari,Kurakatá, pozo Diablo, awiri Tetas.

Ey ʉnza'kinugay eymanke'ri ma'keywa uga powru neyka ʉnhani'kumʉya ni. Zʉnekʉ zanʉ ʉnkʉgachori zoyeykari Magdalena, Cesar awiri Guajira neyka ni.

populate the mountain range of the Sierra Nevada de Santa Marta and are distributed along three Departments (similar to states in the U.S.A), and these are Magdalena, La Guajira and Cesar Departments.

In Nabusimake is where the future is analyzed, and the most important decisions related to the Arhuaco world are made.

Nabusimʉkeri pinnagwi wrunhakumey zoyani ayaba'ri, mʉnʉ́ zʉ́nnige neki inʉ diwʉn niwi kʉnika awʉngwa neki nanu neyka ni.

1.12. PEDAGOGICAL ACTIVITIES

NIKAMʉ

1. Read and analyze the following concept map

YA AWIRI MAPA AWAREY NEYKA WARUHA AWKWA

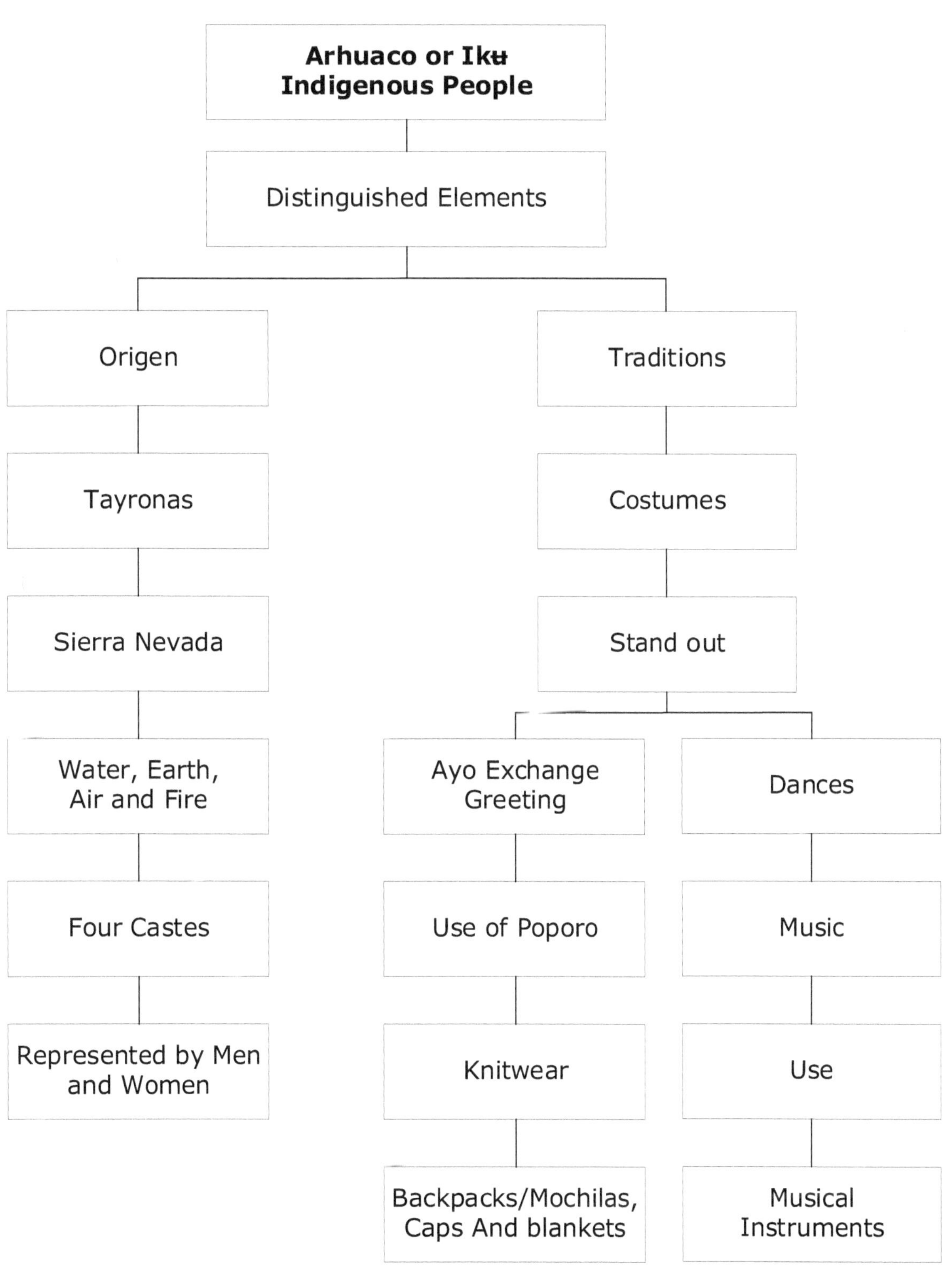

2. Match the Columns.
Write the corresponding letter from Column "A" into the parentheses, in Column "B", that better represents the concept mentioned

Column "A"

a) Gumuku
b) Mamo
c) Poporo
d) Mochila
e) Carrizo

Column "B"

( ) Used only by men
( ) Knitted
( ) Caste
( ) Musical Instrument
( ) Adviser

3. Ideogram
Complete the following chart

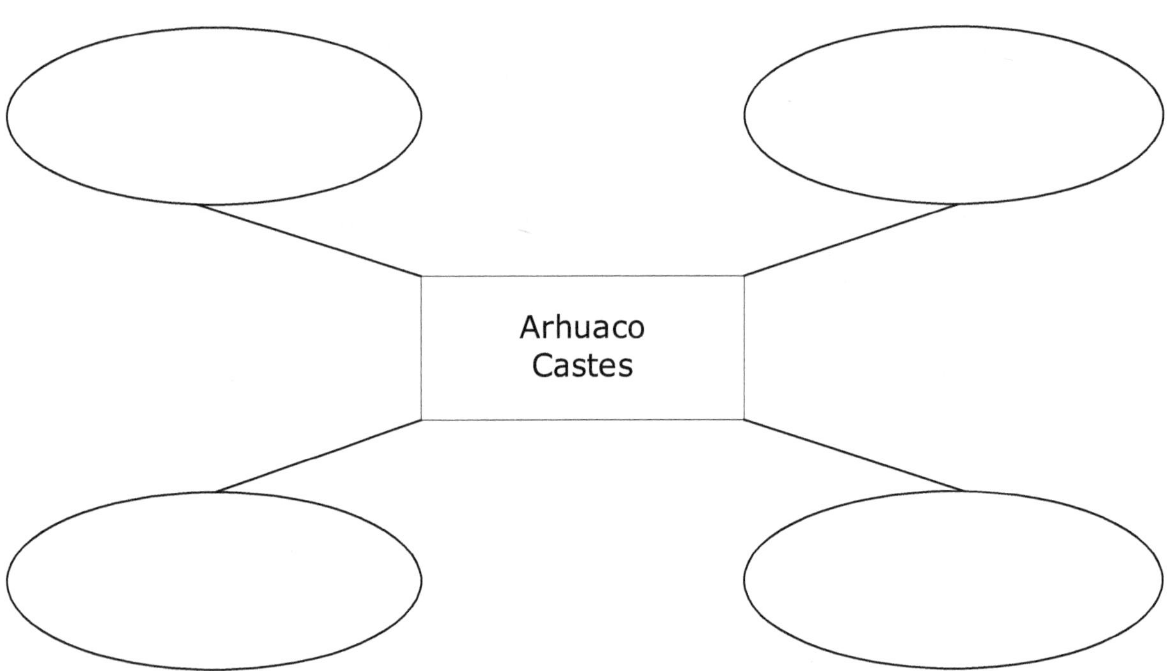

2. MATTER AND ENERGY

2.1. CONCEPT OF MATTER:

Western science has given the name of MATTER to everything we can see, smell, touch and taste. This means that a stone, a backpack, water, air, a piece of cloth, an animal or an orange, is MATTER.

The word matter is used to indicate everything that exists in the universe. That is to say, that the whole universe is formed of matter: the sun, the planets, the clouds, the stars and the moon, are also matter.

Then we can affirm that matter is everything that exists, everything that surrounds us, everything we see and what we touch.

CHUIKʉNʉ AWIRI ɈUMʉKʉNʉ

CHWIKʉNʉ ZAKA'NUGA

Kunsamʉ o'kʉrigʉn zánʉri chwikʉnʉ (Materia) ɉwa kʉsaki nugari manʉnka yow chukwéy, re'busʉkwéy, tosʉkwéy awiri re'kusʉkwéy neyka gunti ey awga ni.

Emari azi zari eyzano awanʉndi in'gwi a'nʉ, in'gwi tutu, ɉe, wamʉ, ingʉ binkin mʉkkʉ, ana'nuga, kwa in'gwi tʉzʉwa chʉmi neykari chwíkʉnʉ nanu nanno.

Chwíkʉnʉ ikʉka neykari emi yow es ka'gʉmʉse' chwʉzʉneyka zaka'chósʉya na ni. Ey awʉndi ka'gʉmʉse' kʉnʉneykari chwíkʉnʉ gunti na' nanno: ɉwi, ka'gʉmʉ ɉina, mʉñʉ, wirako'ku awiri timari chwíkʉnʉse' na ni.

Ey awʉndi, chwíkʉnʉ wasaykwa nanʉndi emi yow ínʉki kwʉyeyka yow niwinminaki nuga, yow chukwéy niwikʉnʉna neyka awiri tosukwéy neyka na' nanno.

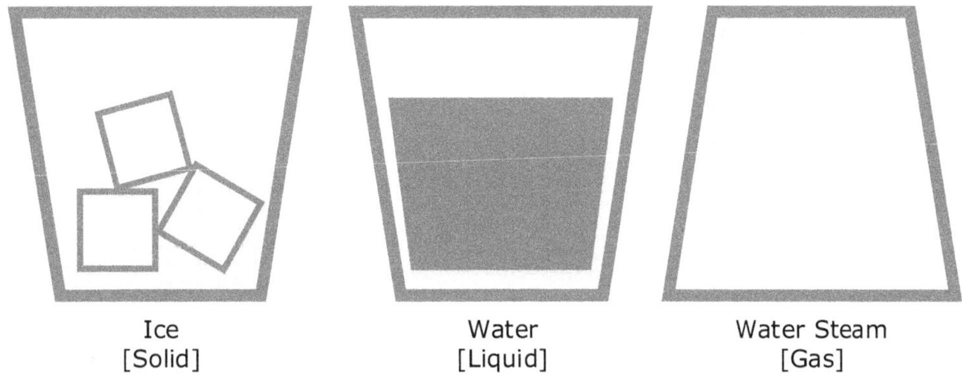

Ice [Solid] | Water [Liquid] | Water Steam [Gas]

2.2. CONSTITUTION OF THE MATTER:

All MATTER consists of small particles called ATOMOS. These atoms are strongly grouped to constitute the body of things.

It is known, for example, that in a bean seed there are millions of atoms. We can then say that atoms are very small particles that are present in all matter to form it.

For example, if we take snail shells and crush them, we will see that they become very tiny white dust particles. This means that the snail shells are made up of dust particles, which in turn are made up of smaller and smaller particles until they reach those minimum particles called atoms.

CHWIKɄNɄSE' KɄNɄNEYKA

Ʉya ɉunari ney nanámʉsin chu' nanʉkwani ʉyari chwikʉnʉsia za'kinuga ni. Chwikʉnʉsiari ɉuma' nisi chwíkʉnʉse' kʉnʉna ni.

Eyma zana, niwigʉnkuyari, ichʉ zʉwase'ri chwíkʉnʉsía sʉmʉ kʉnʉna nani. Ey awʉndi chwíkʉnʉsía wasaykwa nanʉndi umʉngwi ney neyka chwíkʉnʉse' kʉnanʉn nuga in'geygwi nikʉngwa.

Inʉkise' kʉnari zoya na' nanno. Ema zana nanʉndi:

ɉo'tinwʉ ingʉ pey awkwa nanʉndi ʉnpey kumanari ingʉ ey gwi ingʉ kawi gunti wow nari bunsikawi chuzá' nanno; ey awʉndi ɉo'tinwʉri ey gwi ingumʉn ney neyka awiriwow nari bunsikawi kʉnanu nanno.

2.3. COMPLEMENTARY ACTIVITY:

Give other examples about the constitution of matter and draw it.

Also, atoms can be different in form, weight, a sizes.

Thus, for example, in water there are hydrogen atoms and oxygen atoms that make up the matter "water" or H_20 (which means that in each water molecule there are 2 atoms of Hydrogen and 1 of Oxygen). These atoms have different shapes, different weights and different sizes.

NIKAMɄ KAWA'KUMɄNGA

Ʉya zana neyka chuzʉhasi awkwa ni, emi chwikʉnʉ kʉnʉneyka.

Ey unayu nʉngwari chwikʉnʉsiari diwʉ́n diwʉ́n kawa ni yʉkwasi:

Ema zana ɉese'ri chwikʉnʉsiari "Hidrógeno" za'kinuga awiri "Oxigeno" za'kinuga kʉnʉga ni chwikʉnʉsia ɉinari diwʉ́n diwʉ́n kau'nanno, mʉ ɉina a'zʉna'ba awir kawa'ba.

HYDROGEN ATOM

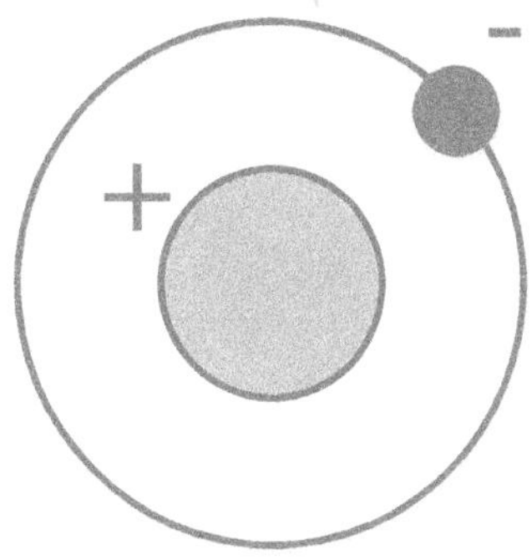

OXYGEN ATOM

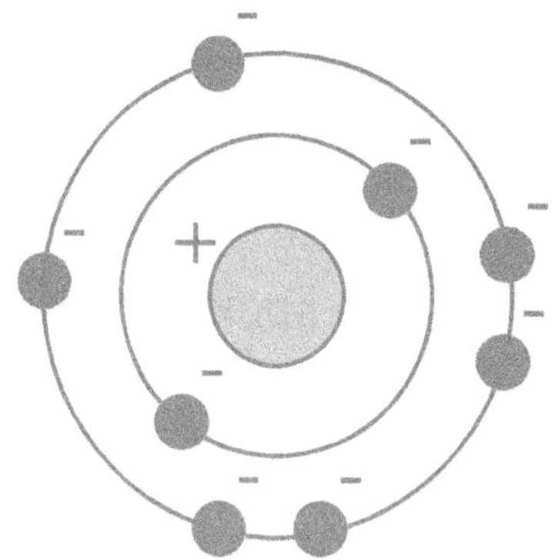

Other elements include ...

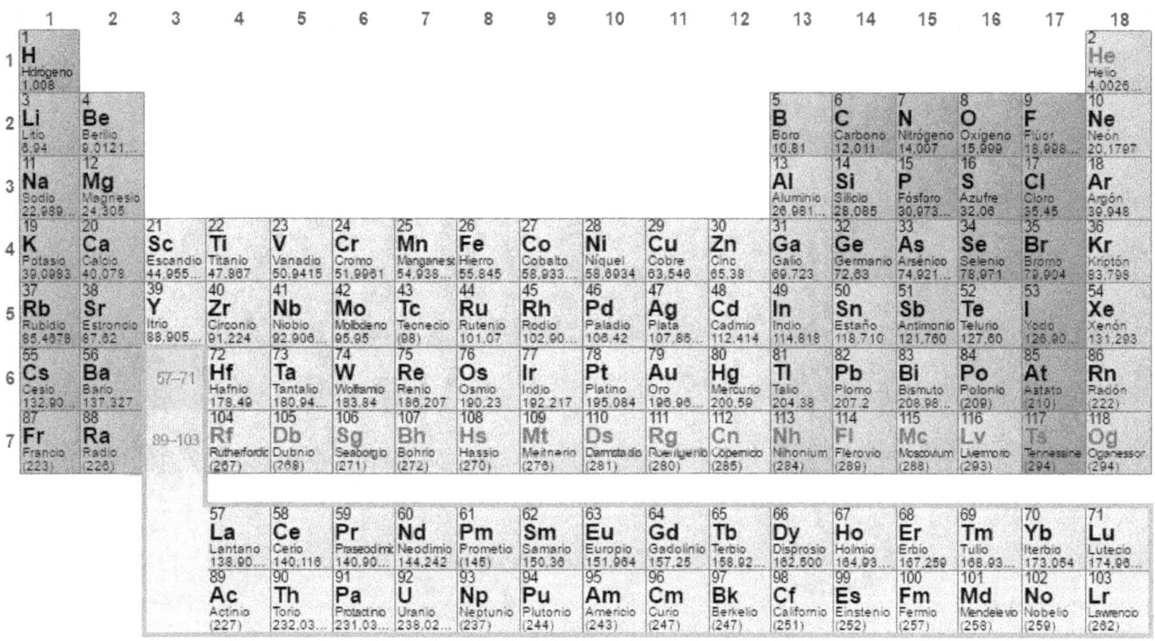

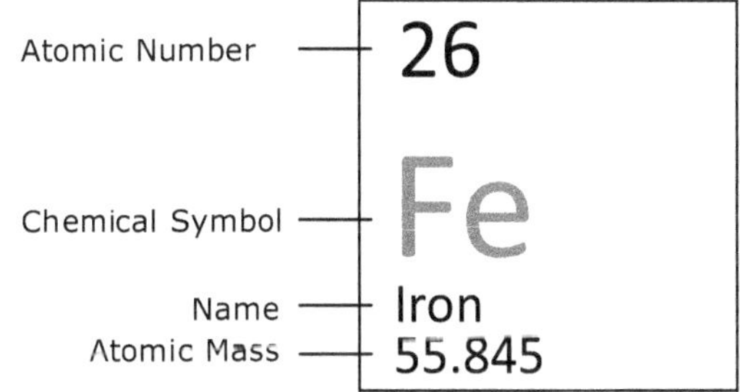

In total, there are more than 100 basic elements in nature

Ema ɉuna neykari uga uga ugámuru nánʉkin wa'kʉzʉna'bari kwʉya ni.

2.4. STATES OF MATTER:

Generally speaking, matter has been classified in three forms or states:

CHWÍKɄWɄ ɈUNA

Chwikʉnʉsía eygumʉn kinki ɉwa'kumʉyeykari máykʉnʉ ɉuna nánʉkin re' basaki nuga ni.

2.4.1. THE SOLID STATE:

This state corresponds to hard and strong things like a panela, a stone, a log, a bone, an avocado or a backpack.

RICHɄ NEYKA ɈINA:

Ema ɉinari inʉkí richʉ neyka ey awga ni. Ema zana panera, a'nʉ, kʉn, wesu, awakati, kwa tutu, ayu ɉinari, richʉ nariri tosʉkwéy gunti na' nanno.

Also the Jaguar and other animals are in solid state.

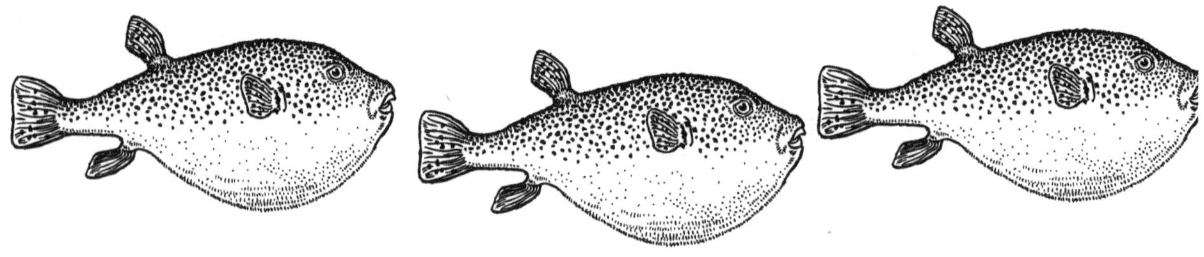

2.4.2. THE LIQUID STATE:

This state corresponds to the water that runs through the rivers, lagoons and seas. The milk that is extracted from the cow also belongs to the liquid state.

ꞰE NEYKA ꞰINA:

Ema ɉina neykari ɉe nanʉn nuga na ni. Ɉe swi, Ɉiwʉ, awiri mʉkuriwa. Tu neki pakase' a'dunna ɉe neykase' kʉtwínuga ní.

2.4.3. THE GASEOUS STATE:
It is formed by clouds, fog, and smoke that comes out of the firewood when it is burned.

WAMʉ NEYKA ɈINA:
Ema ɉina neykari mʉñʉ, kʉgey, awiri zacha kʉn púnʉye' a'chuna neyka ni.

2.4.4. CHANGES OF STATES

In nature, matter constantly undergoes transformations or changes. For example, ice (being solid) may melt and become liquid.

CHWíKʉWʉ ɈUNA ʉNTA'KUMʉYA

Ka'gʉmʉ niwinmi'naki nʉga'bari chwikʉnʉri ʉnta'kunkumey zoya ni. Ɉe ʉnkʉchunna (ɉwabu, ageytʉ, ɉʉn) eygwi ɉe nisi zoya ni.

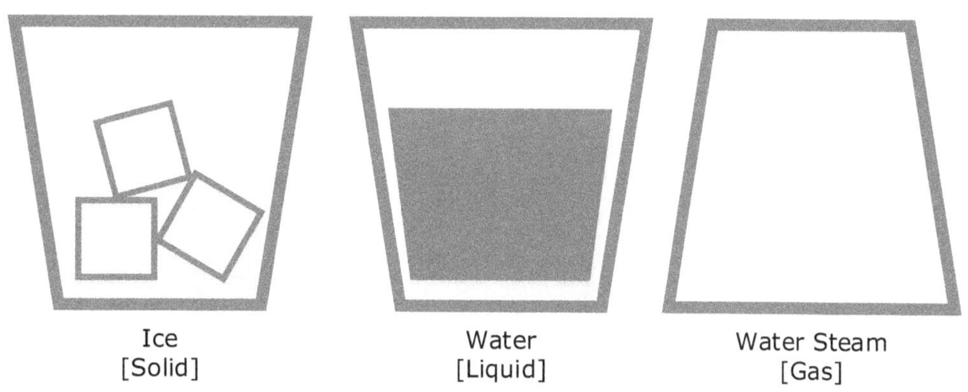

Another example:

Water from a river or the sea can get so hot that, when it evaporates, it becomes clouds (or gaseous form).

Iwa eygwi aykʉnʉri ɉe' swise' zanʉ kwa mʉkuriwari wamʉ nisiri mʉñʉ ʉnniga ní.

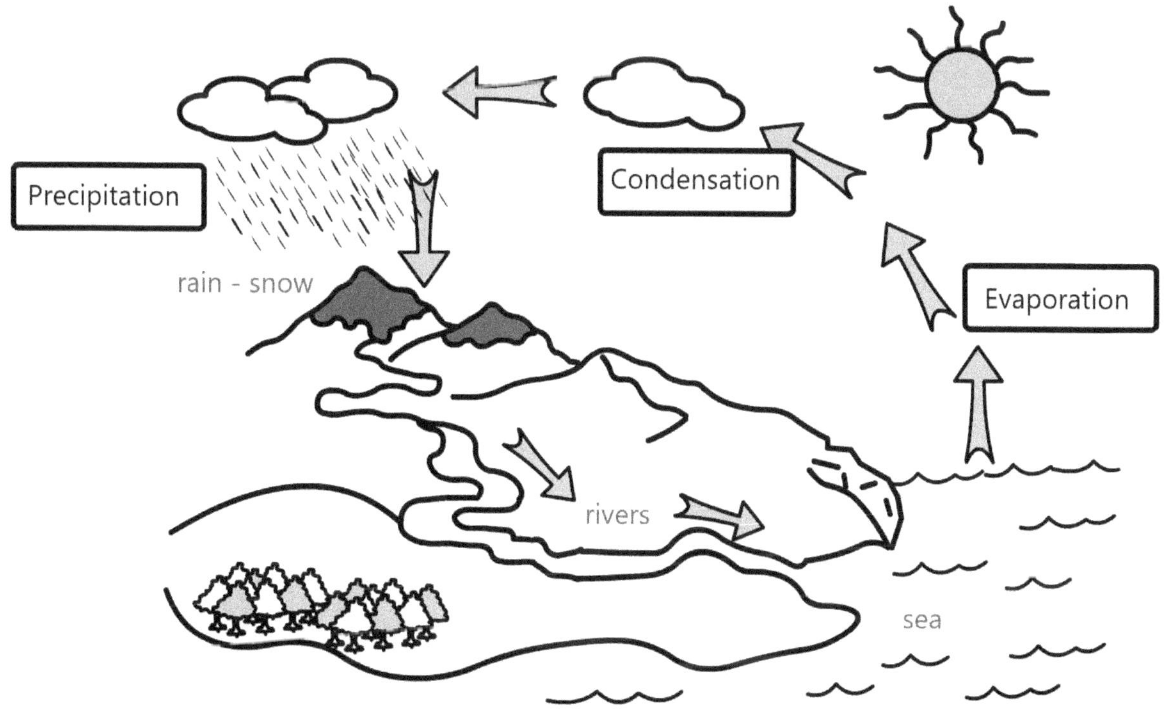

2.5. PEDAGOGICAL ACTIVITIES:
Provide other examples where a change of state is observed.
Try to draw it:

NIKAMʉ
ʉya nanʉ zana neyka eygwi áykʉnʉ eygwi chuzʉnhasi awkwa ní.

2.6. CONCEPT OF ENERGY:

Let's look at the following examples:

The sun can dry clothes.

Fire is able to burn a house.

Lightning can knock down a tree.

This power that the sun, fire and lightning have, is called ENERGY.

We can say then that ENERGY is force, strength, power, or capacity that an element possesses to perform a job or to produce changes in itself or in other elements of nature.

2.6.1. TYPES OF ENERGY

Energy can manifest itself in several ways, for example:

In the form of Heat (fire)
In the form of Light (the sun)
In the form of electricity (lightning)

There are several kinds of energy. Let's see some of them.

ɈUKɄNɄ

ɈUKɄNɄ ZAKA'NUGA

Ema zana neyka chwa úkura:

Geyri urakʉ neki swa awiza ní.

Ɉwitinbiruri kʉn neki wʉsa awiza ní.
Ɉwi, gey awiri ɉwitínbiro eyméy níkʉkwa kʉnʉnari.

Ɉúkʉnʉ (energía) za'kinuga ní.

Ɉumamʉ ɉwise', geyse' awiri ɉwitinburuse' kʉnʉneykari ɉwíkʉnʉ za'kinuga ni.

Ey awʉndi ɉukʉnʉri, ɉumamʉ,

kumʉ, neyka ni yu' nánʉko.
Ikʉri du kawi ɉúkʉnʉ kʉnʉna na'nanno.

ɈUKɄNɄ ɈUNA

Ɉukʉnʉri diwʉ́n diwʉ́n gwi nari achwʉzʉnhasi zoya ni ema zana.

wiwi a' zari (Gey)
A'kisi nari (Ɉwi)
Geysia nari (Ɉwitimbiro)

Emi ʉnchwʉn nusiri ɉukʉnʉri diwʉ́n ɉuna ku' no. Bema no me' zari chwa úkura.

Coal

Nuclear

Hidroelectric

Wind

Solar

Biomass

Petroleum Natural Gas

Solid Waste

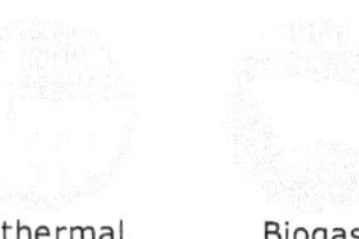
Geothermal Biogas

Hidroenergy low impact

2.6.2. SOLAR ENERGY:

This energy is concentrated in the sun and reaches the earth in the form of light and heat.

This energy can be used for agriculture, to dry clothes, to illuminate, to warm the body, etc.

It can be said that the main source of energy that the earth has is the sun.

ɈUKʉNʉ ɈWISE' A'KISʉYA

Ema ɉukʉnʉri ɉwise' kʉnʉna ni, ʉyari a'kisi awiri wiwi a'zari ka' gʉ́mʉse' kinkumʉya ni.

Ema ɉukʉnʉri ʉnzarikʉkwa'ba, mʉkʉ ʉnkʉ du sʉkwa'ba, niwika'kisʉngwasi awiri gʉchʉ wiwi ʉnkakusʉkwa'ba niwikamʉkanʉkwey niga ní.

Ey awʉndi ka'gʉmʉse' umʉ́n ɉumamʉ kʉnigari ɉwi na ni.

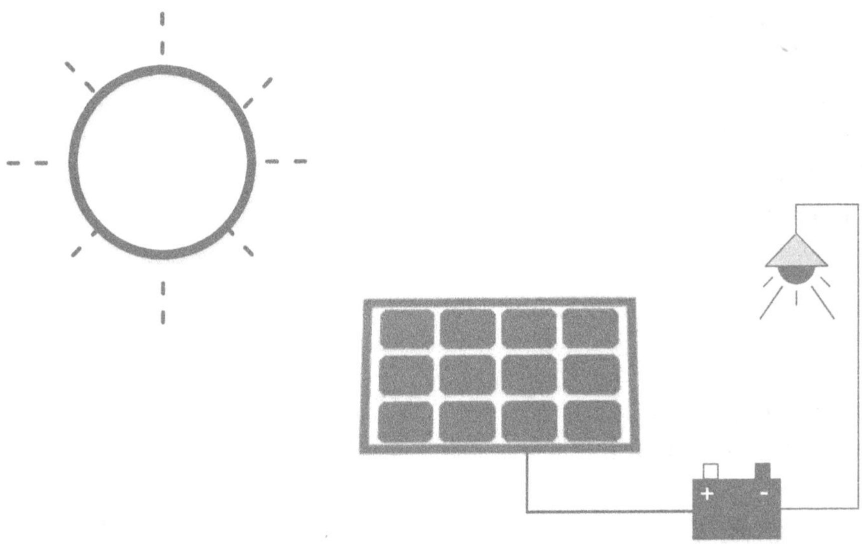

2.6.3. RADIANT ENERGY:

It comes from the Sun and Fires. With this energy you can, among other applications, dry clothes, prepare food or warm up the body.

In the Sierra Nevada, a FOGON is widely used to obtain caloric energy from firewood or coal.

ɈUKʉNʉ WIWI A'ZʉNA

ʉyari ɉwise' awiri geyse' kʉnanʉn nuga ni.

Ema ɉukʉnʉsindi mʉkʉri ʉnkudusʉkwéy nariza ni, zamʉ neki ɉokwa, kwa gʉchʉ kʉmʉ mikakusa awkwey nisiza ni.

Umʉnʉkʉnʉse'ri gey mika'mʉkanʉngwa awkwey niga ni ɉʉ́kʉnʉ wiwa a'zʉna niwi kʉnanʉngwasi.

2.6.4. ELECTRICAL ENERGY:

When it is raining, it is common that lightning strikes the earth. These rays are capable of knocking down a tree because they are equipped with Electric Power.

In cities, electric power is used to operate televisions, refrigerators, stoves, radios and other devices. This energy is obtained from "sources of electricity or power generation".

In the Sierra Nevada de Santa Marta, some towns are able to enjoy electricity thanks to the installation of Solar Panels or from thre grid connected to the generation sources.

But, in more remote locations, the use of solar panels is usually more frequent.

These solar panels collect energy from the sun and transform it into electrical energy.

GEYSIA ɈUKʉNʉ KʉNʉNA

Ɉewʉ wa'nʉye' ri jwitínbiro wa'rizáy na' nʉnno.

Ɉwitinbiruri kʉn neki wʉsa awiza ni ɉúkʉnʉ geysia kʉnari wa'nʉyame' bunachʉ zʉpowrubari. Ɉúkʉnʉ geysiase' kʉnʉnari emi terewisor, newara zaruga'ba, radiw awiri bema neki ka'mʉkanʉngwásʉya na ni. Ema ɉukʉnʉri ʉyase' kinki nari bunna'ba pari winʉkʉnʉna ni.

Niwi umʉnʉkʉnʉse'ri in'gwi powru z̲una'bari geysia ka'mʉkanʉngwá'sʉya ni, ʉyazey kinkumʉya'ba (Panel Solar) ʉyari ɉwise' pari jʉkʉnʉ igusi awiri geysia ʉnnisi zoya ní.

Ema eyméy nisi ʉnta'kumʉyeykari ey méy kawi chuzʉn akumʉya ní.

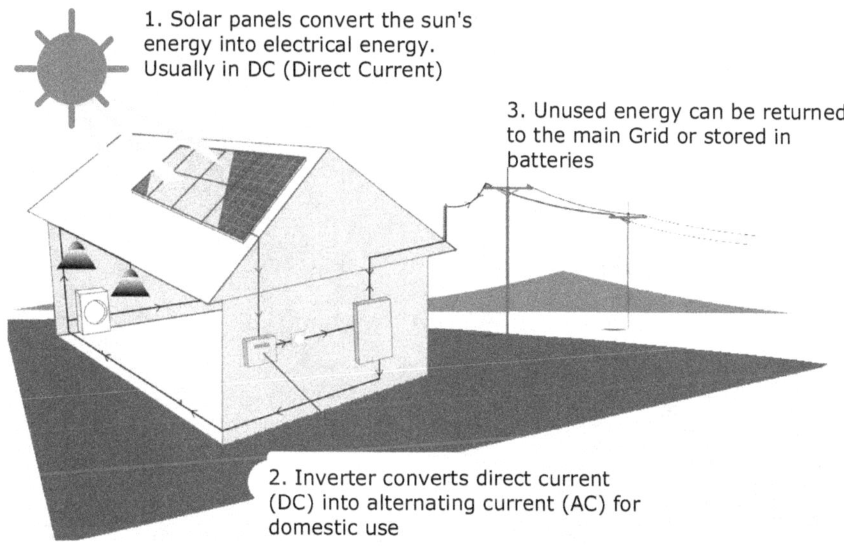

2.6.5. THE HUMAN ENERGY:
Man is a being endowed with a lot of strength, and a lot of ENERGY.

That Energy that man possesses is obtained from the air, water, and food he consumes. If a person does not eat well, he will have less energy.

IKʉ ZʉJUKʉNʉ
Ikʉ nʉnkurari ɟumamʉ niwikʉnʉna ni awiri sʉmʉ ɟúkʉnʉ niwikʉnʉnagwi.

Júmʉnʉ ikʉse' kʉnari, wámʉse' ɟese', ka'se' awiri zamʉ gey ukumʉyase' niwe'wésʉya ni. Ikʉ du zamʉ gu' neykari awʉ ɟúkʉnʉ kʉnʉna ni.

Art by Connie Gomez Lora, used under her permission

2.7. PEDAGOGICAL ACTIVITIES:

Perform the following activities:

1. What is the difference between electrical energy and caloric energy?

2. Where does the energy concentrate in the human body?

3. Interpret through an image the energy that the sun provides to living beings.

4. What damage and benefit cause the electric power in the Sierra Nevada?

5. Why is the sun's energy important in humans?

NIKAMʉ UKUMʉNGWA.

Ema nikamʉ neyka awa awkwa.

1. Be na'ba diwʉn kawʉnno ɉukʉnʉ geysía awiri ɉukʉnʉ wiwi a'zʉna.

2. Ɉukʉnʉri íkʉse'ri bemʉnke mikʉnánʉko.

3. Dibujusin zaka'cho awkwa, ɉwikʉnʉ ɉwizey, chʉká a'zʉna ɉinase'ri azi nisi a'mʉkanʉnno.

4. Ɉwikʉnʉ geysía neykari be na'ba wa'mʉ awiri du nanʉnno.

5. Azi name' ɉwikʉnʉ bunkwakukwizeyri ikʉse´ri chʉwi niggari nanno.

2.8. THE UNIVERSE

THE UNIVERSE (Reading):

The Universe is made up of bodies that shine with their own light called Stars; bodies that reflect sunlight, called planets and bodies that revolve around planets called satellites. There are also smaller bodies such as asteroids, comets and meteors, of which very little is still known about their trajectories and physical composition.

The Sun gathers around itself bodies of various sizes that rotate describing orbits, these are called planets.

The group of bodies formed by the Sun, the eight planets and numerous satellites and astronomical objects that rotate directly or indirectly in an orbit around the Sun, is called the Solar System.

The planets of our solar system are: Mercury, Venus, Earth, Mars, Jupiter, Saturn, Uranium and Neptune.

The planets have several sizes and are located at great distances. In addition, they rotate on an axis and at the same time they circle around the Sun. These movements on their own axis and around the Sun, are known as rotational and translational movements respectively.

YʉKWEYNA

Chʉkímurwari, ka' diwʉ́n diwʉ́n neyka kʉnʉna ni. Ema neykari azey gey kʉnʉna, ʉyari wirako'ku za'kinuga ni, ko' ɟwise' gey íwésʉyé a'kisʉyari ka'gʉmʉ, awiri ka' aɟwa ka'gʉmʉ tina mi'nʉya, ʉyari "satélite" za'kinuga ni, Eymi pari aykʉnʉkʉchʉri, ka'ri umʉ́n ney neyka ayeygwi kwʉya ni, ʉyari asteroides, cometas awiri meteoritos winneyka ni.

Wirako'ku ɟinari acheynanke' ka' ney kwa grʉ neyka ʉnni'si zoya ni, ʉyari azakʉrigʉn, mi'ri, ey ʉweri eyma ɟinarí ka'gʉmʉ awga ni, (Planetas). yow ɟwi, ikawa ka'gʉmʉ kwʉya awirí ka'gʉmʉ ingiti kawa nenʉ́n ʉnni'kumaki nugarí Sistema Solar za'kinuga ni.

Ka' gʉmʉ ɟina "Sistemas Solares" kʉnʉnari ema ni: Mercurio, Venus, Tierra, Marte, Júpiter, Saturno, Urano, Neptuno y Pluton. Ka'gʉmʉ ɟinari in'gwi umʉ́n kawa, in'gwi awʉ winna ni; ey awiri peykʉ peykʉ zʉn winʉnkʉnʉna ni. Ka'gʉ́mʉri a áykʉnʉ mi'ri kéywʉri e' kingwi ɟwi gaka winimí'nʉya ni.

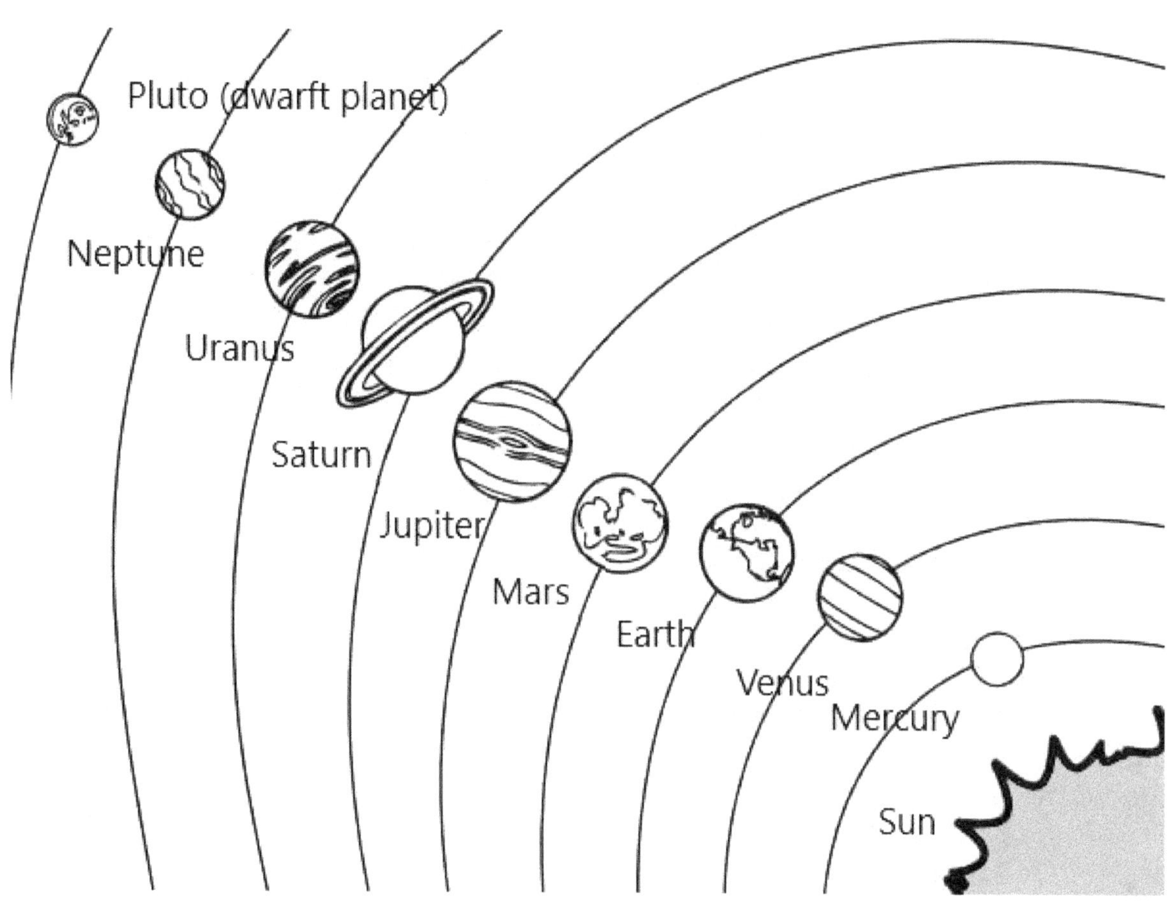

Our Solar System:

Mercury
Venus
Earth
Mars
Jupiter
Saturn
Uranus
Neptune

Pluto was initially considered the ninth planet around the Sun, but it really is a dwarf planet in the Kuiper belt, a ring of bodies beyond Neptune. It was the first object of the Kuiper belt to be discovered around 1930.

Niwizey ɉwi zʉnhumʉnʉkʉ

Ema wirako'ku ɉina ikʉriggʉn neki eykigwi ɉwa neki ka'kumu'gwi ni. Bunachʉriggʉn zʉn ɉwa'kumʉyʉn. Merkuriw, wenu, ka'a, marte, jupite, saturnu, uranu awiri neptunu.

Pluton awgari kʉtʉkʉnʉn keywʉri ikawa naba'ba'gwi kʉnarizay izʉn ne'ki eygumʉngwi ingʉ́ kawámʉsindi eymi par anʉkʉki ukumana ni. Neptunuse' pari eygwi yamʉnkʉchʉ gun nanʉndi.

The forces that keep the planets in their orbit are considered gravitational forces, centrifugal force and centripetal force.

Since ancient times man has been concerned with knowing other planets and, through Technology, has managed to invent instruments such as the Telescope that allows him to observe the celestial bodies at great distances. The largest telescopes are placed in special places called astronomical observatories.

One of the most powerful and highest resolution telescopes in the world is the Great Binocular Telescope (LBT), which is located at the Mount Graham International Observatory, located in Arizona, USA, and is equipped with instruments of great precision to measure the light intensity of each star, calculate distances, sizes, photograph striking aspects and study special phenomena. Other instruments that this type of telescope has are the photometer and photographic devices.

Usually, photographs taken from spacecraft are sent to the ground for study. This has allowed us to know data about the Sun and our planetary system.

Ka'gʉmʉ ɟinari mowga ɟʉna mi'nukweyna kʉnʉna ni "Rotación" awirí "Traslación","Rotación" awgeykari a áykʉnʉ mi'nʉye', ɟwi "Traslación" awgari ɟwi gaka animi'ri zoye' ey awga ni. Ka'gʉmʉɟina mi'nʉn gwa'sʉyari; kumamʉ jumʉ a'nikwʉyekʉ zʉ'n zʉnana ni ʉyari "fuerza gravitacional" zaka'cho'kumu' no; ʉyarí ɟumamʉ "Centrífuga" awiri ɟumamʉ "Centrípeta", ema mowga ɟuna ɟumamʉ neyka kwʉyame' zʉn, ka'gʉ́mʉri ʉya'ba ta kinki ʉnmi'ri zoya ni.

Birin pari Ikʉ arunhey ukureykari umʉ́n ínʉki aɟwa ɟwa'kumu' neyka re'tasi zoyanari zʉname' iwari umʉ́n peykʉ wa'kʉn mígwa'sʉkwa neyka "Telescopio" za'kínuga winachunhaki nuga ni; ʉyari warin wirako'ku, tima kwa aɟwa ka'gʉmʉ neki chwʉkwéy kʉnanʉn gwa'sʉya na ni. Ʉyagwi ne'ki umʉ́n wa'kʉkwey na' nikʉkin wa'kʉn gwa'sʉyari, áykʉnʉ kinki, ʉya kumʉyekʉ Observaciones astronómicas ayekʉ chó'kumey zoya ni.

Ema, peykʉ wa'kʉn migwa'sʉkweyna umʉ́n ɟumʉ kʉnʉna neyka in'gwiri MONTE DE PALOMAR (E.U) ayekʉ kwʉya ní, Ayari umʉ́n pinna ɟuna ka' in'gwi aɟwase' kʉnari zoya, kʉríwin migwa'sʉkwéy neyka; gey a'kísʉya, bin peykʉ winʉnkʉnano awanʉkweyna, ingʉ́ kwa grʉ nʉneyka nenʉ́n, ínʉki ɟwa'sunari arunhá me'kusʉkwey neyka naríkʉchʉ kéywʉri ɟwa'kumu'

This information allows scientists to determine size, shape, temperature, humidity, physical and chemical characteristics, conditions of matter, biological conditions and other characteristics, of other astronomical objects and the relationships between them.

neyka zʉn zoyeyka nenʉ́n yow migʉnchonʉn gwa'sʉkwéy nʉneyka eymekʉ ni. Ʉɉwa ayeygwí nari a'mʉkánʉya "Fotómetro" awiri "aretratu" ʉga chúnʉya eygwi nani.

Warin "retratu" ʉgachunhey ʉweykari eygwí emí anakwʉya'ba ʉnga'kumʉya ní; ʉyari du kinki kʉrigawín gwasi. Yow eméy awi birin wazweín nugeykari ɉwi kwa yow ka'gʉmʉ sí umʉ́n kʉrigawin niwigwa'sa awaki nuga ni. Umʉ́n winarunhʉya ɉina ayeygwi bin kao, azi kao, wiwi zano, kwa za' no, umʉ́n ɉe' kʉnari zoya kwa na'no, ɉina azi kawa no, kwa chwʉzari awa'ba nenʉn azi kawa no ʉwari pin sekʉnanʉkwéy gunti kʉnari zoya ní, ema ʉyéy awkweyna ey winʉkʉname'.

2.9. THE UNIVERSE: IKUN TRADITIONAL CONCEPT:

In the Iku culture, the Solar System is made up of nine floors from the earth down. Each floor is of a different color and belongs to different Mothers.

To move from one floor to another, special permits must be made by making offerings or tributes to each site.

As the floors are passed, circumferences are found, something very similar to the location of the plants in our solar system.

In the IKUN solar system, from the bottom up, the first floor corresponds to KAMUNSA.

When a task requires compliance with all traditional rules, offerings must be paid from our floor all the way to where KAMUNSA is.

Currently, offerings or tributes are made to nine planets.

In the Iku culture the universe encompasses everything, from the ground down and from the ground up, with stars and all the celestial bodies.

The Mother of the Sun is called WITARINNATI and the sun is called BUNKWAKUKWI. The Universe is shaped by these celestial boides and UTIBUNNA (Polar Star), UKWU (the Magi),

IKʉN A WIRI BUNACHʉ SI GA'KʉNAMʉ KWʉYARI

Niwi kunsamʉ siri "Sistema Solar" awgeykari, emi niwika'gʉmʉ ʉndérigʉn re'nikwʉyʉkin gwi neyka ʉyawar ni, ʉyari ikawa na' nó. I'ngweti nʉneykari diwʉ́n diwʉ́n si kʉkumáy kau' nó, (zi', chʉmi, twi kwa bunsi); ey áwiri ʉyari azey azey gwi zaku winikwʉya ni. Tikʉrigʉndi i'ngwi re'nikwʉyʉn pari ʉɉwʉn ʉnkʉzagichʉkwasirí enʉnay narigwi ízasánʉkwa kau'nanno. Ingiti ʉnkʉzagichi re'nikwʉyáy zweykwa nanʉndí mín mín kawi zoyaki nuga ní. Warín ka'gʉmʉ winʉkawaí ayeygwi kawa.

Niwi kunsamʉ siri kʉtʉkʉnʉn keywʉ ka'gʉmʉ ʉnpʉnkwʉyarí KA'MʉNSA za'kinuga ni; ey ʉweri ʉyari aykʉnʉgwi apáw ikwey zwei'nó. Ey ʉwe'ri Mamʉrigʉn keywʉ a'buru kowkumʉpánʉye'ri nʉkínkʉchʉ tina akwʉya'ba pari ka'mʉnsa síkʉkin íazasari wazoya ni. Iwari yówkʉchʉ ikawa ka'gʉmʉ neyka ízasari wazwei' no.

Niwikʉnsamʉrigʉn a'bori una sírigʉndi pin ínʉ chwʉzari ʉwa neyka Ka'gʉmʉ chʉkímurwa (Universo) awga neykari, emi akwʉya'ba pari kʉtʉkʉnárigʉn awiri yow ku'nawakin wirakó'kusin, ɉwisin, timasin aɉwa ka'gʉ́mʉsin pínkʉchʉ ʉya gʉnti niwikizʉna ni.

MONUKUNU (Star that shines a lot in the early morning) and NAMTYAWIKU who were women of the Sun.

JWIKASINTANA is the Mother of everything that exists, so the various ethnic groups have the same places of tribute; the only thing that changes is the names due to the corresponding ethnic group (Arhuaco, Kogi, Wiwa or Kankuamo).

Ɉwi zazákuri WITARINNATI za'kinuga ni, iwa ari BUNKWAKUKWI.

Ka' gʉmʉ chʉkimurwari ema ɉina ayeygwí kʉnʉna ni, UTIBUNNA (estrella polar), ukwʉ (los reyes magos), MONɄKɄNɄ (estrella que brilla mucho en las madrugadas) y NAMTɄAWIKU (que eran mujeres del sol).

ɈWIKASINTANA: Pinna chwʉ zarí ʉwa neyka zʉpáw na ni, ey ʉwame' niwi ikʉ nʉnkureykari iba'kin zʉ'n zasari azoya ni, nʉkin diwʉ́n diwʉ́n zʉ'njwa ɉwa niwika'niku' nanno.

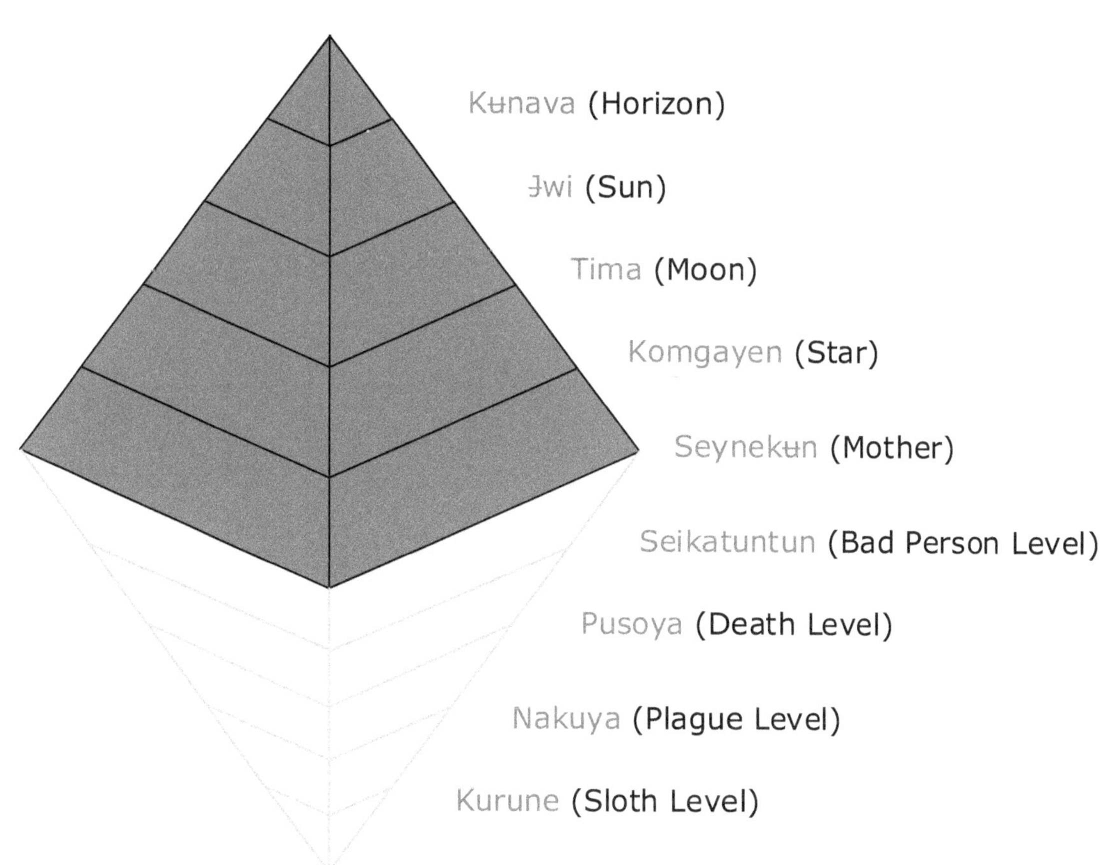

2.10. PEDAGOGICAL ACTIVITIES:

What is the relationship between the BUNACHU (or Western) concept and the IKU concept about the Universe.

NIKAMɄ

Ikʉ zʉ kunsamʉsí nasin Bunachʉ zʉ kunsamʉ sí neykarí ka'gʉmʉ chʉkímurwa sí waséykumey, ga'kʉnamʉ bema'ba mʉchéy ʉnkʉnisi zoyo me'zari du sekʉnánʉkwa.

2.11. TRADITIONAL IMPORTANCE OF THE SUN:

The Traditional name of the Sun is "BUNKWAKUKWI", which is very important for the Iku People.

Let's look at some of those characteristics that make the Sun such an important entity.

The Sun travels in a year from one point to another. In some cases, we realize that the day is shorter and the night is longer; and in other cases, the opposite occurs, the night is shorter and the sun rises a little earlier.

There are two very important times, San Juan and Easter, not in the sense of celebration as we think today, they were considered as the times when the Sun is waiting for the humans' tributes and celebrations.

Humans are responsible for paying tribute for the Plants, the Animals and everything that exists on earth. And this tribute, or payment, is offered to the Sun, since it is He who is illuminating everything, and gives us his energy for the development of the Flora and Fauna around us.

He is seeing everything that happens, and judges the payments and activities of humans. It is Sun who determines whether a long

ꞫWI MAMʉRIGʉN A'MʉKʉNA:

Ɜwiri, mamʉrigʉndi "Bunkwakukwi" za'kinuga ni. Niwikunsamʉ síri du kwi a'mʉkʉneyka zakʉka'nuga na' no. Ey ʉwe'ri in'gwi ɟuna zaka'cho' awʉndi.

Ɜwiri kʉgi zʉnʉkin i'ba nikwana'ba pari in'gwi eygwi áykʉnʉ ʉnniga ni. Ey ʉwe'ki iwrui diwʉ́n nari dʉmʉna ni, du chukwa nanʉndi i'mʉnʉri ɟwia'rí umʉ́n ko'kó zánikunó. Iwa neki ʉyeyki niku'nó. Ɜwiri mʉnʉ' nayʉn nʉngwa a'zʉnasin mʉnʉ'gwi áykʉnʉ ʉnniku' no. Sanusi ʉnnʉnáy nanu' nari.

Mowga ɟuna zeywamʉ ʉnkumʉya kwʉya ni, San Juan awiri Semana Santa, ey ʉwe'ki zeywamʉ ʉnsi kweákʉchʉ awi neki za'nari, ɟwi a'buru kanikʉngwasi aɟwín wa'kʉn nugame', pin ikʉ nʉnkureykase'.

Ikʉ ánugwe niwikéy ʉwa neykari pinna ɟuna aná'nuga, kʉn awiri yow chwʉzarí ʉwa neyka, apáw ɟinase', a'buru kawi kinki zweikwey niga ní, ɟwiri a'kisʉn nusi keywʉri, yow zarí ʉwa neykarí chwʉn nuga ni.

Ɜwiri niwe'zasisa ʉwa ni, tikki kwa ɟewʉ nekí ʉntʉnhey zoye'ri, wichamʉ, zamʉ tikumey, pinna ɟuna aná'nuga kwa kʉn wichi zoye'ri; ema yari eyzano e'zanʉndí, ikʉ arunʉkwa kawi na' nanno (ikʉ, bunachʉ pinna)

summer or winter should occur; its consequences, diseases, food shortages, and if other limitations must occur.

Today we realize the variation of weather that causes imbalances in nature. The summer months exceed the months that corresponded to it, rain decreases and water sources dry out or their flow get reduced.

Another important aspect is that the Sun has an influence on women; so when a girl develops into a woman, the Sun cannot see her until the Mamo performs all the ceremonies and recognizes her as a new woman, as another member of humanity. From then on, the Sun will always consider her throughout her entire life.

enʉnay ɉwi kʉzusi uzwei' name' , na' nanno.

Iwa né sekʉnánʉkwa nanʉndi chwágʉmʉ za'nó, diwʉ́n diwʉ́n zarí zʉ'n ɉwi nʉyáy zari, pinna ɉuna aná'nuga kwa ikʉ nenʉ́n ʉnkʉre'kumáy zari, emi ka'gʉmʉ tina' ʉndeno'kukwa na'nu nari, tikki keywʉ nʉge'ri eygumʉ́n kinki ɉomʉ zʉn' awi ɉwi nay zoyaygwi, du ɉewʉ ʉnwa'nu' ne'ri beki ɉe'cho' zari zoyari ʉya ʉndu'ri zʉne kínkiri ɉe nʉkin kʉchʉ tikumey zoyáy niku' no.

ɉwiri niwichwʉya ne'ri, ayéy kinki izasari uzwei' nanʉndi yow wa'mʉ sí awkwo sí'gʉn ánugwe niwikʉnikundi yow ase' mʉ kazániga ni.

SUN

2.11.1. MEANING OF THE SOLAR ECLIPSE:

ɈWI RIGɄYE' ZAKACHO'KUMɄYA:

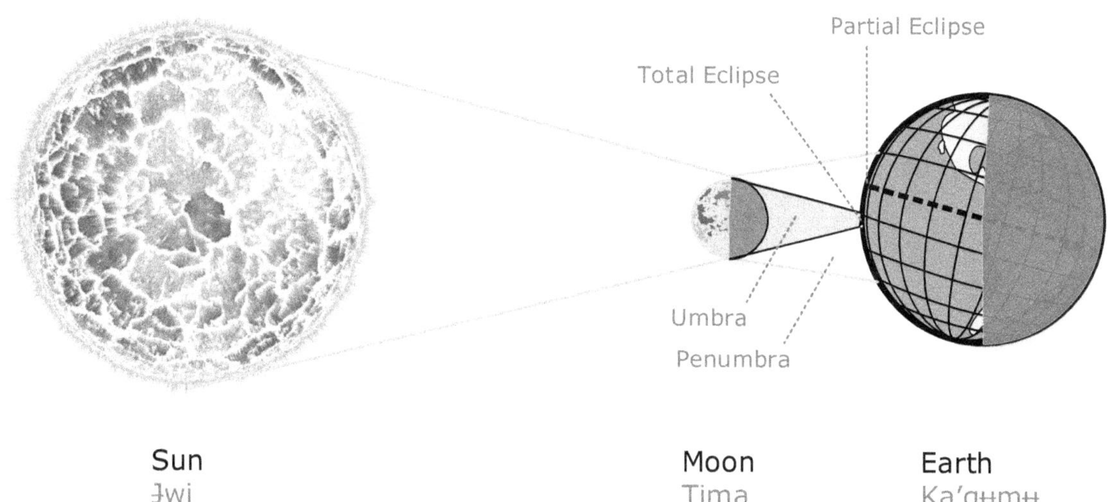

Sun
Ɉwi

Moon
Tima

Earth
Ka'gʉmʉ

It is worrisome when this phenomenon occurs, because all humanity is affected. It occurs when there is no understanding and there is an imbalance with our environment. Diseases and pestilences arrive as envoys from the river, invading all species of nature.

Emey zari (ɉwi rigey) zoye'ri ikʉ nari nankwa'bari yow wa'mʉ zari chuzániga kawi neykani. Emey zánigari ʉnkʉnpanu nari awiri gugin ʉnkazanu nari zeykwase' zʉna ni. Wichamʉ ɉunari ɉeswí neykase' unakay nisi, zʉnekʉ a'pʉgeri zweínpʉna ní, pinna chʉká a'zʉna wa'mʉ a'si.

In the Arhuaca culture, the solar eclipse means the intimate act of love between the Sun (as a male being) and the Moon (as a female being).

Ikʉ arhuaku nʉnkura'bari emey zari zoyeyka awgari Kakʉ Bunkwakukwi awiri zaku Bunkwanowasin i'ba nari winʉnzasanʉn nusi eyzʉnaní awga ni. (winde'riguzari)

2.11.2. MEANING AND IMPORTANCE OF THE SOLAR RING:

ɈWI ZɄSOMɄ AGUGEYKA AWIRI A' MɄKANɄYA.

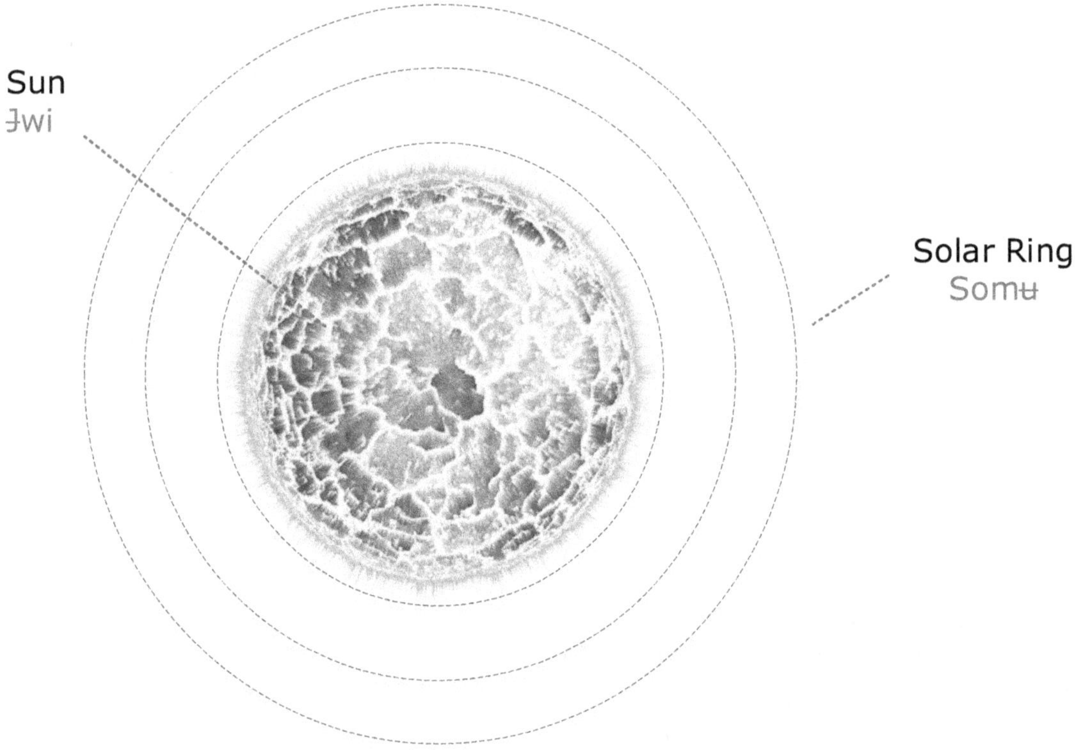

The solar ring is a circle that sometimes appears around the Sun. It can have different shapes and, depending on the case, could have different meanings:

a. That during the day there will be heavy rains that can cause damage.
b. That diseases are approaching, therefore, tributes must be made.
c. That it is a good time for planting.

The traditional name of the solar ring is SOMU or SASOMU. And it is the Mamo who will be in charge of determining the meaning of each Somu.

Ɉwi zasómʉri min kawi churo ɉwise' i'mʉnʉ né ʉnchó'sʉya ey awgin. Diwʉ́n diwʉ́n kawi achwʉzʉna sʉye'ri, ʉyari i'ngweti azey azey gwi zaka'nuga ni:

a. E' ɉwiase'ri du kawi ɉewʉ wanámʉsin tʉnha awʉngwasi ey zʉna ni.
b. Wichamʉ kumʉ a'nisi naka awʉngwasí, ey ʉwe'ri ʉyari mamʉrigʉn péykʉgwi chwʉkwa niga ni.
c. Ingʉri du zaríkʉkwa zanʉngwasi ey zʉna ni.

Ema eméy ɉwi chʉro ʉncho'sʉyari niwiga'kʉnamʉ siri somʉ kwa na' nandi SASOMɄ awga ni.

2.12. PLANET EARTH:

MIWIKA'GɄMɄKA'

It is the planet on which we live and is located in the Solar System. It has a spherical shape and flattened at the poles, almost like the shape of a chicken egg.

The Earth (or Ka'gumu) is made up of a gaseous part called ATMOSPHERE, composed of Air, Breeze, Clouds and other components in a gaseous state. For a liquid part called HYDROSPHERE, formed by the Seas, Rivers, Lagoons, Underground Water, Ice and Snow. And, for a solid part called LITOSPHERE, formed by Mountains, Hills, Stones and Rocks that make up the surface of the Earth.

Ema ka'gʉ́mʉri niwi akwʉya kinki ey awga ni, awiri emi aɉwa ka'gʉmʉ ɉina richwʉzanʉn nuga'bagwi chwʉ zʉna ni. Ey ʉwerí min kawiri emʉn emʉn asakʉrigʉn ʉnkʉtwí twi kawa ni.

Ari wamʉ neyka ATMOSFERA za'kinuga kʉnʉna ni, ʉyari wamʉ anʉ́mkʉsi awkweyka, búntikʉnʉ awiri mʉñʉ awánʉkwa gunti na' nanno. In'gwi eygwi neykarí ɉe' na ʉyarí HIDROSFERA za'kinuga, éymiri ɉiwʉ, ɉe' swí awiri mʉkuriwa. Aykʉnʉ eygwi akowna neykari richʉ neyka LITOSFERA za'kinuga ʉya'bari kʉ́nkʉnʉ, gwírʉkʉnʉ, a'nʉ awiri a'timoku ʉwanʉkweyna gunti rinanʉn nuku' nanno.

2.12.1. EARTH MOVEMENTS:
Planet Earth has two main types of Movements:

The Rotation Movement and the Traslation Movement.

The Rotation Movement produces the effects of day and night lasting 24 hours.

This movement can be compared with the one made by a spindle when spinning.

The Translation Movement is the one that makes the Earth around the sun, having a duration of 365 days.

The path that the Earth travels during the Translation is called ORBIT.

This movement has an effect on the arrival of the SEASONS (winter, spring, summer and autumn).

In the Sierra Nevada de Santa Marta, winter and summer are primarily considered for agricultural activities such as planting and harvesting, as well as for everything related to Traditional tasks. For example: tribute is made during droughts, or during wildfires or for harvest. Offerings are made so that summer does not harm living beings. Also so that winter does not harm the farm, crops, animals and humans too.

KA' MI'RI AWA NEYKA SIRIGʉN
Ema ka' gʉmʉri mowga ɉuna mi'namʉ kʉnʉna ni:

Mi'namʉ "ROTACION" aguga neyka awiri "TRASLACION":

Mi'namʉ "ROTACION" agugeykari ɉwía' awiri seía' zakusʉn nuga na ni, ʉyari mowga uga ma'keywa kʉtów hora' zane' yow mi'ri zoya, ey awga ni.

Ema mi'ri ʉwa neykari kurkʉnasin ʉnkʉwákʉkwéy na' nanno, beki si burenʉn nuge'ri.

Mi'ri awkweyka "TRASLACION" awgeykari ka'ri ɉwi animi'ri zoya ey awga ni, emari ɉwi yow animi'ri, aykwárigʉn ana'chona anʉwe'ri, 365 (máykʉnʉ uga ugámuru chinwa uga asewa kʉttow) ɉwia' zʉne' yow mi'naki nuga ni.

Ingunʉ ka' mi'ri zoyeyka TRASLACION awgeykari ORBITA za'kinuga ni.

Eméy nisi ka' ʉnmi'ri zoye'ri diwʉ́n diwʉ́n zákusi zoya ni, tikki zakusagwi, ɉewʉn zakusagwi, awiri i'ngwi aɉwʉn zʉneykari; OTONO, yow kʉnachʉ wa'ri zʉne' iwa PRIMAVERA aye'ri yow kʉn tínzizey kʉnachʉ du kawi ibónʉye'. Ema tikki awi ɉéwari ka' ʉnka'nikʉn gwa'sʉkwa'ba se rekʉnánʉkwey niga ni. Tikkise'ri chey ʉngawkwa, ʉnzaríkʉkwa iwa ɉewʉndí ananikʉye' ʉnʉnkʉtákʉkwa', yow ema nikamʉ neykari ánugwe nari

The other two seasons, spring and autumn, are not very marked or observable in the Colombian Caribbean region.

ayeygwi aykʉnʉgwi mamʉrigʉn ɉwi kʉzusi chwʉkwa niku' nanno.

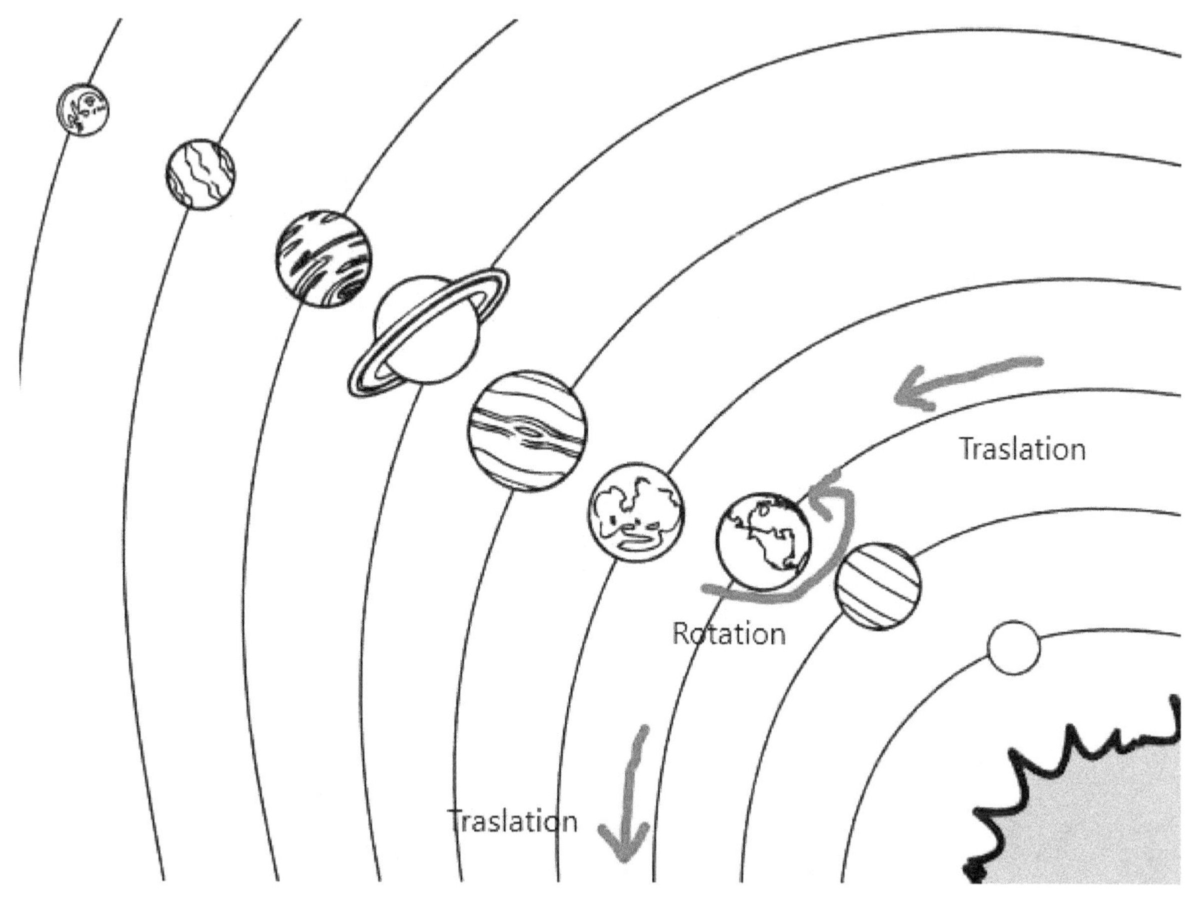

2.12.2. SEISMIC MOVEMENTS: According to Iku tradition, our Mother SEYNEKUN left four men to carry Earth on their shoulders. These strong and powerful men called SEYMUKE have sustained it from the beginning and for this to continue, offerings must be made. When the KAMUNSA or earthquakes occur, it is because the traditional law has not been fulfilled and then the spiritual cleansing and offerings must be done to be at peace with our Creator Fathers.

Earthquakes will have a particular meaning according to the time they occur. And again it is the Mamo who will be in charge of determining the meaning of each earth tremor.

In BUNACHU (or Western) thought that movement is known as Tremor, Earthquake or Telluric Movement; and occurs due to the movement of underground tectonic plates or layers

KA'MɄNSA ZARI ZOYE' Niwizaku Seynekʉndi ma'keywa ikʉ, kwi'se' ka'gʉmʉ igekwʉngwa nari chusana na' no. Ema ikʉ rinanʉn nugari ánugwe nari peykʉ ɉumʉ a'nisi, agʉ́mkwʉya nanʉn nʉga SEYMɄKE za'kinuga na ni, ey ʉwe'ri birin pari akínkingwi nasi ka' gʉ́mʉri azi niku' nari zweingwásiri tʉyéy kinki nʉnʉkin mamʉrigʉn chwʉkwa nisi zwei' nanno. Beki ka'mʉnsa keywʉ kínkumey zoye'ri apáw sikʉ enʉnaí kínki a'buru kanisi azwei' name' na ní. Ey awʉndi ʉyari azey azey gwi apáw íkwʉya name' ayeygwi nari izasánʉkwa kau' nanno.

Binzari ʉyéy ka'mʉnsa kinkumʉndi, ʉyarí ayase' togwi chwʉkwa tikkʉrigʉndi kawiza ni.

Bunachʉ zʉkunsamʉ sirigʉndi ema ka'mi'ri ʉwa neykari · "Temblar" "Terremoto" kwa "Movimientos Telúricos" ɉwa winʉka'nikwʉya ni.

Seymʉke

2.13. THE MOON (Traditional History):

The Moon was created by KA'KUNMAKU and PUNA MEYNUN. They took good care of her and didn't let her out for fear that someone would steal her.

When many people came to sing to the Fathers, the Moon took advantage and fled behind the Sun. She was already far away when the Fathers realized and then they threw ashes in her face, and that is why her light is not as clear as that of the Sun. The Moon still followed the Sun and did not come back.

The Moon is a carrier of much knowledge. She also has an influence on women, by producing physiological changes, such as mood and menstrual cycle.

The Moon is the wife of the Sun and they visit each other once a month.

TIMA (Kunsamʉ ikʉrigʉn)

Timarí ka'kunmaku awiri puna meynʉn apáw nari kwʉngwa re'gowna ni. Ari du achwiri use' pari a'chonʉn gwa'kumu' nʉnna ni, azageyza chow izari. Re'masi ikʉ aɟwa ɟina apáw.

Ka' zamayʉn anase'ri, eméy zanʉn núkʉkindi ɟwi zʉtʉkin kurenika una ni. Peykʉ ʉnzwein nuse' keywʉ apáw ɟinase'ri ke winʉwʉnna, ey uye' nʉngwari búnzʉga keywʉ kʉwitʉrinna; ʉyari umʉkʉna' a'pʉgere' neki ɟwi a'wasi kingwi zoya unáɟuri naku' nʉn una ni. Eméy nari búnzʉga a'pʉgeri una name' ɟwi narí kawi neki a'kissu na ni.

Timari ayeygwi du kawi kunsamʉ agʉ́nkwʉya ni. Ʉyari a'mia sírigʉn waseykumʉya ní, ey ʉwame' eymari ɟwi zʉnha'mía náriri, tima zʉne' ʉnte windinachwʉya ni awga ni.

MOON

TIMA

2.13.1. THE PHASES OF THE MOON AND ITS RELATION WITH TRADITIONAL ACTIVITIES:

The Moon has four phases and in each of them different traditional activities are carried out.

TIMA DIWUN DIWUN NIGE' A WIRI E' NIKAMʉKʉ UKUMʉYA

Timari ma'keywámuru nánʉkin ʉnta'kunkumʉye'ri, ayeygwi azey azey gwi nari nikamʉ ɉunari awkwey niga ni.

2.13.1.1. NEW MOON

TIMA AGʉMʉ

On this phase, the moon represents an optimal time to treat some illnesses using massages or to treat a fracture.

Children and adults can also be given laxatives, as it is considered that more parasites are expelled at this time than in any other phase of the moon.

Tima agʉmʉ nanʉn nuge'ri re 'pinsi awkwa du neyka ni, ema timase'ri bema bema gwasi umʉ́n zi witésʉkwéy name'.

Ey ʉwame'ri wichamʉ sírigʉn rinachukwa ayeygwi du neyka ni, beki ʉntwisi awkwa, kwa re' seri mikizʉnna nandi asirisi du re'kusʉkwa.

2.13.1.2. FIRST QUARTER

TIMA INAYʉN NUGE

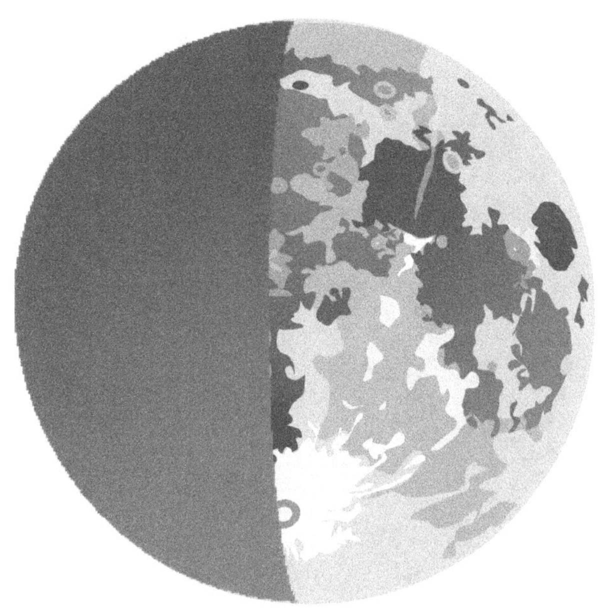

During this time, the Moon has grown a quarter of its size and the other part remains dark.

It is a good time to plant some crops, and so does it to treat diseases.

Iwame'ri (Ey ʉwame'ri) timari nʉkin ineyna neki na' na dikin na'nʉkin inʉyaki nuga ni, iwa in'gwi eygwi dikin neykarí chwʉzanu' nari churo' inuga ni.

Ey ʉweri ema timase'ri in'gwi kʉn zaríkʉkwa du neyka ru, wichamʉ chwi zweykwa du neyka ni.

2.13.1.3. FULL MOON: TIMA YOW CHWʉZʉNE'

Now the moon is completely round and illuminated. It is when it "shines" the most, or reflects the sunlight at night.

It is good time to seed all kinds of crops, and it is expected to produce good harvest. It is also a good time to castrate animals as it is expected they will not bleed much.

Emiri timari yow nʉkin chwʉ zári'ri nukin a'kísʉya ni. Seía'ri umʉ́n kinki a'kisʉya ni.

Emiri pinna ɉuna zamʉ ínʉki bonʉkweyna zaríkʉkwa du neyka ni; eygwiumʉn du kawi a'nikʉya name'. Beki aná'nuga ʉnwʉ a'kwisʉkwa ayeygwi, a'yari ʉwame' ʉmʉngwi ɉwa witesu' na ni.

2.13.1.4. THIRD QUARTER

TIMA ʉNWICHʉYE

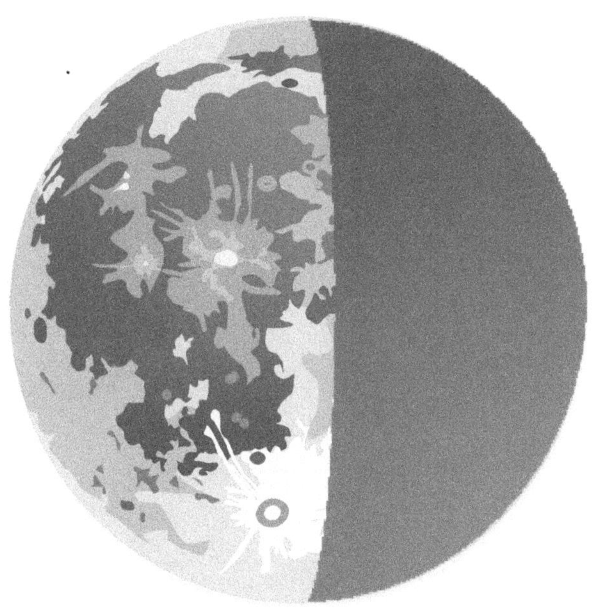

After the full moon, little by little the moon begins to decrease its size. And its only illuminated in a quarter of its size, while the rest appears dark. It is said then that the Moon is in the phase of THIRD QUATER.

During the phase of the Waning Quarter, the wood must be cut to build the houses. This wood would be more resistant to moth and termite and also very strong and durable.

It is also a good time for the collection of grains such as coffee, corn and beans; because weevils are not expected during this time.

Tima yow chwʉzʉnna nariri, eygwi ɉwmʉ ɉwʉndí ana'yuri ʉnzoya ni. Yow neki na' nari dikin zʉ'n ɉwise' a'kisʉye'ri Cuarto Menguante bunachʉ sírigʉndi awga ni. I'ngwi eygwi neykari gumʉ aniyú zʉ'n neyka ni.

Ema timase' tima ʉnwichʉn nuge' kʉn urakʉ bonʉngwari beykumʉya ni. Ey ʉwame' kʉn beykumanari rigu' gwawa neyka ni awiri beki karo'ru kwa zise' gu' gwawa neyka ni, eméy anawʉyame' umʉ́n richʉ ki nʉngwi awiri umʉ́n a'mecha ki awagwi zʉ'n ʉwa ni.

Anazari'na anʉnkʉtákʉkwa ayeygwi du neyka ni, inʉ ne gwákʉkwa nanʉndi Kafé, In, Ichʉ; emari ema timase' ata'na ne'ri kunse' neki gu' na ni.

2.13.2. MEANING OF THE LUNAR ECLIPSE.

TIMA RIGʉYE ZAKA'NUGA

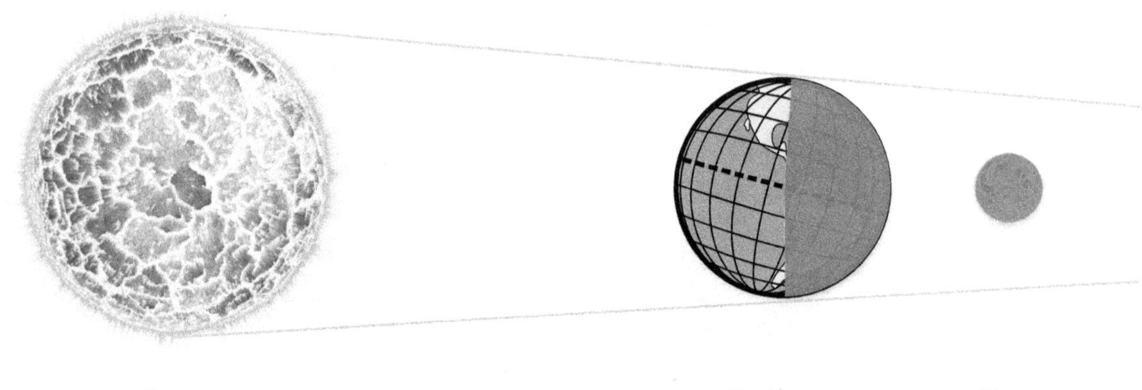

Sun
Ɉwi

Earth
Ka'gʉmʉ

Moon
Tima

The Moon Eclipse is a natural phenomenon that occurs when the Earth, our Planet, stands between the Sun and the Moon. When this occurs, Earth's shadow completely obscures the Moon.

In the Arhuaco tradition, this event among the stars signifies the birth of women, as well as for the plants will to produce excellent harvests. The same goes for animals that have Young breeds, those will develop without any problem.

Finally, we would say that the Moon indicates the fertility of women and other meanings that only Mamos and Elders have the ability to recognize.

Tima riga ʉwin ikure'ri ɉwi nariri timasin winʉnka'nikwʉyʉn niwi ka' gʉmʉ bʉkʉna nika ʉwame' ey awgani.

Eméy zʉneri, ka'gʉmʉ zʉchuro'ri tima gumʉ iyu awi ɉwi a'zániga ni:

Niwi kunsamásiri, eyméy zʉne'ri a'mia winneyka kwakumʉngwasi ey zʉna ni, kwa kʉn ɉuna neki du kawi zamʉ a'nikʉngwasi. Ayeygwi ana'nuga a'miasí zaká'nuga ni, ʉya ɉinari agʉmʉsinʉ anʉ a'nusi, azi a' zanu' nari kʉnanʉngwa name' ey zʉna ni. Aya ni.

Ey awʉndi tima waseyniwiza nanʉndi, timari a'mia zʉzayʉn neyka na' nanno, ay awi keywʉri eygwi umʉ́n, mamʉ ɉina, umʉnte kʉzʉna ɉina se'ri winwásʉya na'nanno.

2.14. PEDAGOGICAL ACTIVITIES:

Complement your knowledge by developing the following activities.

1. Make a concept map about the phases of the moon.
2. Represent on a cardboard the phase that you usually observe and share it with your teammates.
3. Research with your parents. What is the phase of the moon suitable for planting crops?
4. Ask your grandfather. What happens if we cut wood for construction in a crescent moon? Why?
5. Describe in detail what happens when there is an eclipse of the sun.

NIKAMɄ

Ema nikamʉ awʉn nusi eygumʉn kunsamʉ kawʉnka'sa awkwa.

1. Mapa conceptual awga gow awkwa, tima ʉnta´kumey zoya sí.
2. Kartulinase' tima ʉnta´kumey zoyeyka gow awkwa.
3. Mikakʉ a'zasisa awkwa. ¿tima bemay nʉnnige zamʉ zarikʉkwa du nanno?
4. Mizʉrʉmakʉ a'zasisa awkwa. ¿tima agʉmʉ gekwánige' kʉn urakʉ bonʉngwa beysʉndi azi nikʉnno.
5. Zachʉn a'sa awkwa ɉwi rigey zoye'ri azi zániga no.

FLORA AND FAUNA IKʉ

3. FLORA

3.1. GENERAL GOALS

Rescue and preserve the value of the Arhuaco's ancestral knowledge related to their study of plants, the importance of plants in everyday life and their traditional classification according to their use and spiritual Ikun laws.

Highlight the importance of conserving natural resources (plants), in order to allow better sustainable development for current and future generations.

Know some of the general characteristics of the plants and classify them, according to their properties and their use.

KʉTʉKʉNʉN RE'NIKWʉYʉN: KʉN ɈUNA

EYMEY KʉZARI EMARI A'KUMANA NI IZANʉNGWA NEYKA.

Anizátikumana neyka anʉnkʉtasi awiri ɉumʉ kʉssi, kʉn ɉuna sí riwí ʉnzori; ema sí ikʉse' sigín ka'mʉkari ʉnzoya'ba ey awiri kunsamʉ sírigʉn re'bákumey anʉwa'ba, anugwesin ana'mʉkari ʉnzoyame'.

Ikʉ anʉwiwya ɉinari ʉnchwʉzari awʉyeyka kwa kʉ́nkʉnʉ anʉka'mʉkari ʉnzoya'ba ɉumʉ kʉssi zoyʉngwa, ey unige'ri abiti ɉinase' ʉnwinʉka'mʉkana awkwey nikʉngwasi kunsamʉ niwikʉnʉnáy anʉkʉriwín nuga'ba.

Emari a'zanʉn gwa'sa awiri ɉwa'sʉn gwa'sa, a'mʉkanʉya sí. Emi chwʉzari awʉyeyka riguzʉnhasa awiri azi nari kwakumana no me'zari ʉnɉwa'sʉn nusi, ey anʉwa'ba pari kʉchonʉn neki gwa'su' nari ʉyagun niwiánugwe awiri niwigʉchʉ ɉumʉ niwikʉsʉya name'.

Bema kʉn nenanki re'nikwʉyáy anʉkʉɉwa'si awkwa'ba zanʉ neyka.

3.2. HISTORY OF ORIGIN (Reading)

In the beginning, everything was dark; there was only water, the sea was everywhere. The sea was the mother of everything there would be later. Everything that exists today was in her womb. Then, she saw the need for material elements and life, and that was when Bunkwakukwi sent strong thunders, and everything took color, shape, size, and spirit. Thus, according to the Ikun law, the mother determined each element to each being.

Then, there was people too, but not of the same race. Each race was giving a spiritual law to transmit education to their children and to discuss with others; a unique language of its own, which shall be taught with according to their traditions.

Unfortunately, many tribes began to forget their duties and choose to adopt the laws of others. Then, these tribes were chosen to provide a more useful service to human kind.

RIGA'WIYA'BA UZORI UKUMɄNGWA NEYKA

Niwi niwe'zʉneykari, umʉnte a'zʉna ɉinase' (gʉmʉsinʉ zʉpáw, mamʉ, gunamʉ, sakuku) a'zasíkumey nanʉn nuga'ba riwiya ɉinase', emakin nanʉn nusi ukumana'me,
ema chwʉyase'ri ʉnɉwa'si kinki zweykwa.

Riwiyase' ema ingiti a'kumey wazoyanari winʉkuriwi uzoriri, ema imʉ neki nanu' nari, bunachʉ sírigʉn akingwi kʉɉwa'si zweykwa ni.

Kwadruse' kʉn pinna ɉuna re'bakumanari gʉmʉsinʉ awí zoyase' ʉmʉ́n awkwéy kʉnanʉngwasi, ey anunige'ri re'riwiya ɉinase'ri paperise' yow a'sʉn gwa'sa neki au' nari, ema zana ni yʉkin kʉnikʉngwasi, ey anunige'ri riwiya ɉinase'ri kʉn diwʉ́n diwʉ́n zʉnekʉ zanʉ awiri kwʉyʉn zanʉ winɉwa'si nanʉngwasi.

Ema waséykumʉn nugari gʉmʉsinʉ awiyase' ka'mʉkari zweingwasi, ase' ʉnɉwa'si anʉwa'ba pari umʉnte a'zʉna wina'zasisʉyasin umʉ́n kʉriwiwkwéy winʉkʉnikʉngwasi.

For example, there were members who always showed affection for healing others, so the mother gave them the power to become medicinal plants. Other members asked to be converted into ceremonial elements and the mother saw this need, granted them power and laws for their conservation.

Furthermore, the same happened with many other things.

After several years, the mother find it necessary to establish laws for food, and created the edible plants, establishing laws for their use according to the time, place, ceremonial, community, family and individual use.

BIRIN ZANɄ: KɄN ɈUNA KWAKUMANA (a'gwakʉkwasi)

E' kʉtʉkʉnʉndi sein zʉ'n zʉnna ni, ɉe zʉn kwana, mʉkuriwari pinzʉnáy a'kwana. Ari pinna kwakumʉngwa
neyka zazaku nʉnna, yow iwa ʉnchwʉzʉneykari zakuse 'ri ase' zʉn kʉnʉnna.

Ey unari, tʉ́kindi ínʉki tina' chwʉzʉnhasa awkwey na' nanno a'zari nʉ́ngwari kwi'magwe ʉ́ncho'naɉu ɉwitinbiro Bunkwakúkwizey wʉ́sana ey uye'ri yow ínʉki kaweyka, nʉ́neyka keywʉ́ chwʉzʉnhasana ey uye'ri azey azey kunsamʉ́ keywʉ́ winʉ́nkʉ́basana.

E' kínkiri ikʉ áykʉnʉ zʉ'n anʉnna, diwʉ́n diwʉ́n a neyka, zákuri kʉnsamʉ azey azey chusana, ʉyari gʉmʉsinʉ winamʉsesʉn nugase' winʉnkawi ey zweingwasi, aɉwa
ikʉsin winderimasayʉngwasi, awiri gʉgʉkʉnʉ azey azey gwi chusana. Ʉyari kunsámʉse' a'nikwʉyáy
winderino'kwʉngwasi. Ey anunari in'gwiri akunsámʉri ʉnchusi zweinpʉnna, aɉwazey ɉumena ikwákumey zweinpʉnna; ey uye'ri eyma ɉinari áykʉnʉ ingʉ diwʉ́n nari
a'mʉkanʉngwasi agagu'na, in'gwiri ínʉki du re'kusʉkwazey aguzanáy nisi achwʉzʉnasana. Ey uye'ri zakuse'ri ʉya sí kunsamʉ a'wena (wichamʉ sí).

A Mamo named Najunna brought the plants. This wise and venerable old man traveled to the afterlife in search of his wife who had died and he wanted to see her. Upon arriving at the place where his wife was, the spiritual parents indicated that her spirit was secured in a pot of covered mud.

Iwa in'gwi eygwi aykʉnʉri mamʉrigʉn a'mʉkanʉngwasi achwʉzʉnhasana. Ey uye'ri ayéy kunsamʉ a'we ukumana. Kʉn aɉwa ɉuna neyka ikwʉngwasi.

Ey unáɉuri birin ʉnzanise'ri, zákuri: "ínʉki gʉkwéy neyka kwasa awamʉ kau' nanno", a'zare'ir, kʉnɉuna gʉkwéy neyka kwasa una, ʉyari diwʉ́n diwʉ́n a'mekari wazweingwasi (i'ngwiri mamʉ sí, use' agʉngwa, pówruse' kwʉngwa).

The spiritual parents told Najunna that, in order to take away his wife's spirit, he had to stay a long time there performing activities such as cutting firewood, cleaning farms, and building houses for his in-laws.

Kʉn ɉuna neykari mamʉ Najunnase' keywʉ una'na, eyma mámʉri achuná kawi kunsamʉ agʉ́nkwʉya gun nare'ri azwei' nʉnárigʉn keywʉ zoyana. Ʉnha'mía zʉnhánugwe ɉwéruse' gumʉ inisi wazoyaki nugame' ʉnkʉtakʉn zoyana. Eykʉ a'chore'ri ánugwe zʉpaw ɉinari – mazey a'míari zʉnhánugweri ɉwéruse' gumʉ a'pʉnsi du ukumaki nugin - kʉyana.

Then, to start these activities, he went to cut trees in the forest and every time he hit a tree, loud cries of pain were heard, the same happened when performing other activities; this meant that the work should not be done materially but in a spiritual way, and then he did so.

Nʉnkuzoyaki awiza nanʉndi sanusi kʉn biwkwa, wagawkwa, urakʉ gawkwa mikau' nanno wʉ'gwe keynakʉ - kʉyana.

Then he decided to return to the place of origin, but before that, he decided to bring plants of all kinds with him. He considered these plants necessary for human life.

That is how he took seeds of all plant and species and brought them around us. Unfortunately, this was seen as an act of theft by the mother, and was therefore persecuted by the spiritual guardians.

Najunna with the desire to protect the seeds, fled; separating life and death in two.

Thus, after this origin, plants began to play an important part in human life.

Nʉngwari keykumanáy keywʉ nikʉnpʉnna, kʉn bin keywʉ zoyana, kʉnkʉnakʉ a'chori beysiwa keywʉ a'zare'ri, kʉndi mawáy keywʉ yʉnpʉnna, áwiri aykʉnʉ níkʉkwa keykumana, uwa a'zare'ri ayeygwi zʉ'n yʉnpʉnna. Ey uye'ri nikámʉri tina'aiuna tikʉrigʉn zʉ'n awkwa nʉnna; ey uye'ri ayéy anunajʉ nʉngwari aykwárigʉn ʉnnaka uwa a'zʉnna, ey awe'ki kʉn pinna ɉuna a'mʉkʉna ikʉ keynakʉ kʉɉuna uzoya uwe du na' nanno a'zʉnna. Eyméy nari keywʉ zaɉuna pinna ɉuna una'na, ey uye'ki anugwe ɉuna zʉ'n,

Najunna taught the story of plants to the members of his community, while was able to receive guidance from the spiritual mother, thus creating laws for the care, use and conservation of the species.

kominsariwse' zagʉn nuga awari, wasa keywʉ winowna.

Najunnari zaɟuna ikwa uwa a'zanʉn nusi íngʉnu kʉwi una kwʉkwa awiri wíchʉkwa re'basa una. Nakʉbirʉ kʉwi'na, zoyʉbiru zʉ'n chusi. Eyméy nari keywʉ kʉn kwákumey ikʉse' ka'mʉkanʉnpʉ́nna.

Najunnari eyméy nari kʉn ɟuna kwakumana ni. Agunamʉ ɟinase' awiana, eyméy gwi nari zakuse'ri kʉn a'we una (kʉnsamʉ), ʉyari ayéy ʉnkwazweingwasi chusana, chwi awiri chow a' chwi azweingwasi.

3.3. IMPORTANCE OF PLANTS

Before the spiritual mother, all living and non-living beings are equally important, we are all related and in need to serve each other. The Iku people have been chosen by the mother to take care of all natural resources.

Plants are resources widely used by mankind. We are the ones who benefit most from them. They not only serve us as food, but also to satisfy other necessities in daily life, such as building houses, cure diseases, to dye, to pay tributes, etc.

That is why we have a duty to take care of plants, protect them with spiritual cleanings and offer tributes to the spiritual mother as an act of thanksgiving for what she has given us.

KʉN ƗUNA A'MʉKANʉYA

Emi pinna ɨuna ka' gʉ́mʉse' kwʉyeykari, zaku ɨinasindi akingwi a'zʉnkura ni. Ey ʉwame'akingwi kwʉniwiza ni. íkʉri pinna chwʉkwa nari zakuse'ri a'guna ni.

Kʉn ɨunari ikʉse'ri akingwi a'mʉkanʉn gwa'kumʉya ni. Manʉnka'ri umʉ́n kinki niwi ka'mʉkʉna na' nó. Ey ʉwe'ri zámʉse' zʉn neki niwi ka'mʉkanu' neyka na' nó, ayeygwi áykʉnʉ diwʉ́n nari niwika'mʉkʉna ni, urakʉ gawkwa'ba, wichámʉse', si kʉsʉkwa'ba, ʉnzasanʉkwa'ba nari gunti a'mʉkʉna ni.

Ey anʉwame' ayéy chwamʉ niwikawa na' nó, chow a' chwamʉ tikʉrigʉndi kunsámʉse' anikwʉyáy zaku sikʉ izasari, ʉya gun niwichwʉn nuga na' nanno ʉwari izasanu' nánʉko.

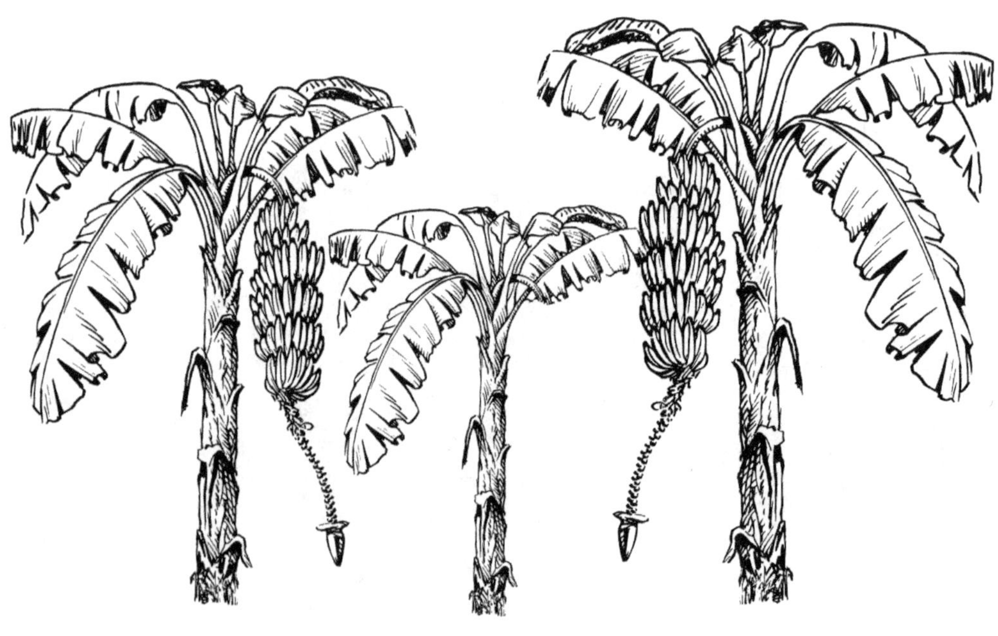

3.4. PARTS OF A PLANT

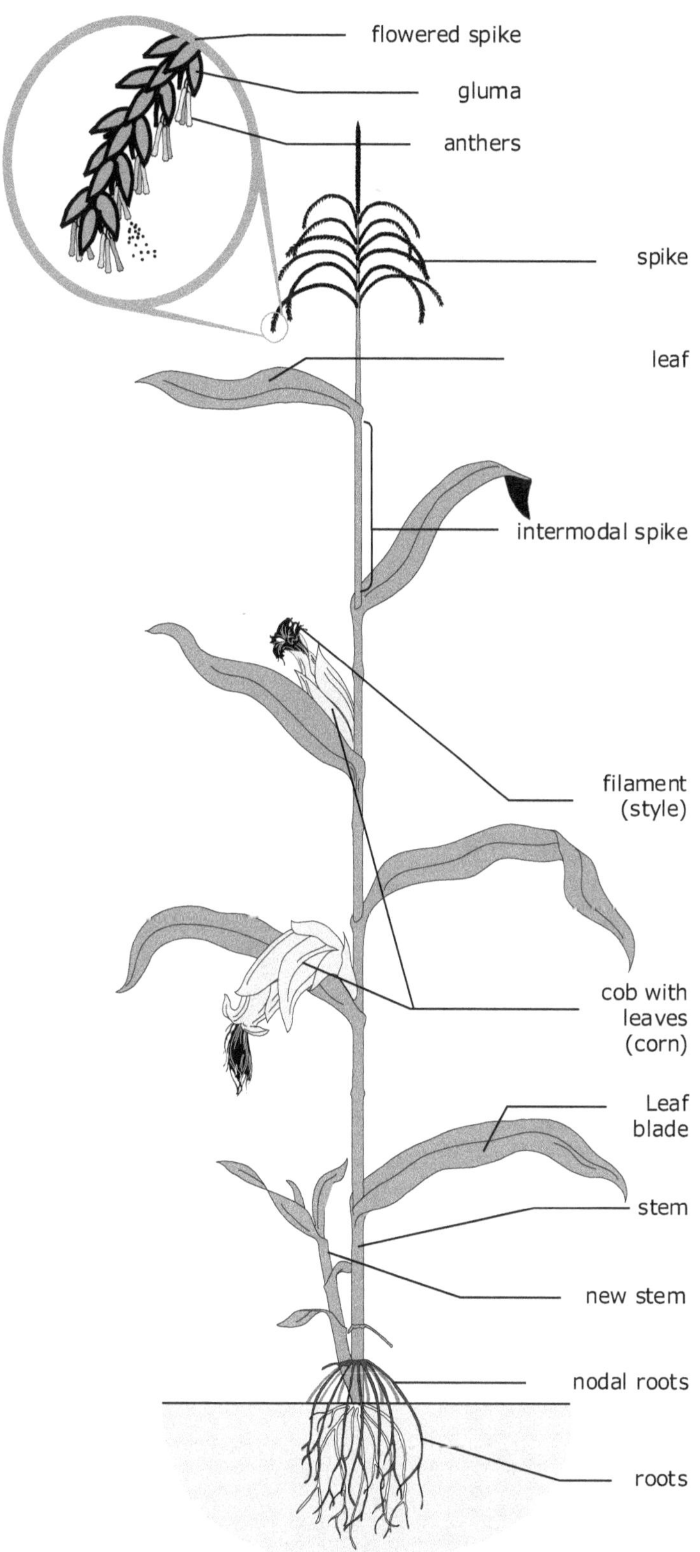

Just as our body is composed of head, trunk and extremities, plants have some parts that form them, these parts are of vital importance for their survival.

Niwigʉchʉ re'nikwʉyáy sakúkusin, goɉírisin; awiri kʉtʉsin nʉnaygwi, kʉndi ayeygwi kawi re'nisi zoya ni, ʉya ɉunari peykʉ ka'mʉkʉna, emi kwey angwasi.

Roots:

They are in charge of absorbing the nutrients that the soil possesses. In addition, they also hold the plants firm to the ground or soil.

Akʉttʉ

Akʉttʉri emi zamʉ ɉuna ka'gʉ́mʉse' kwʉya gusi ʉwa ni, awiri wa'nu' nari a'nukʉngwasi.

Stem:

It is like the bridge that allows the circulation of substances to all parts of the plant. It is also the structure that stores the nutrients that allows the plant to grow, bloom, create more leaves, etc.

Akʉnʉ

Ayeygwi puenti zana' nari zamʉ ʉnkʉzagisʉn gwa' sʉya na ni, re'nisi zoyáy, aya'bari zamʉ du ʉnkáwʉya ni, umʉ́n inayʉngwasi, tinzʉsʉngwasi azachʉ ʉnta'sʉngwasi.

Leaves:

Leaves are very important in a plant because through them the plants breathe. There are small pores called stomata, through which oxygen and carbon dioxide are exchanged, these two main gases are used during photosynthesis and cellular respiration.

Some plants store water in the leaves, and then use it when they need it.

Azachʉ

Azáchʉri peykʉ kʉnse' ka'mʉkʉna ni, be' aya'ba pari anʉ ʉnkʉsʉya gunandi, azachʉse'ri manʉnka zana anʉ ʉnkʉnsʉya kʉnʉna ni, ʉyari bunachʉ siri "estoma" winguga ni, ey anʉwe'ri ʉya'ba tá anʉ ʉnkʉsʉya ni. Ʉya'bari ɉe' du ʉnkawiri anʉkʉjúnʉye' ʉnguga ni.

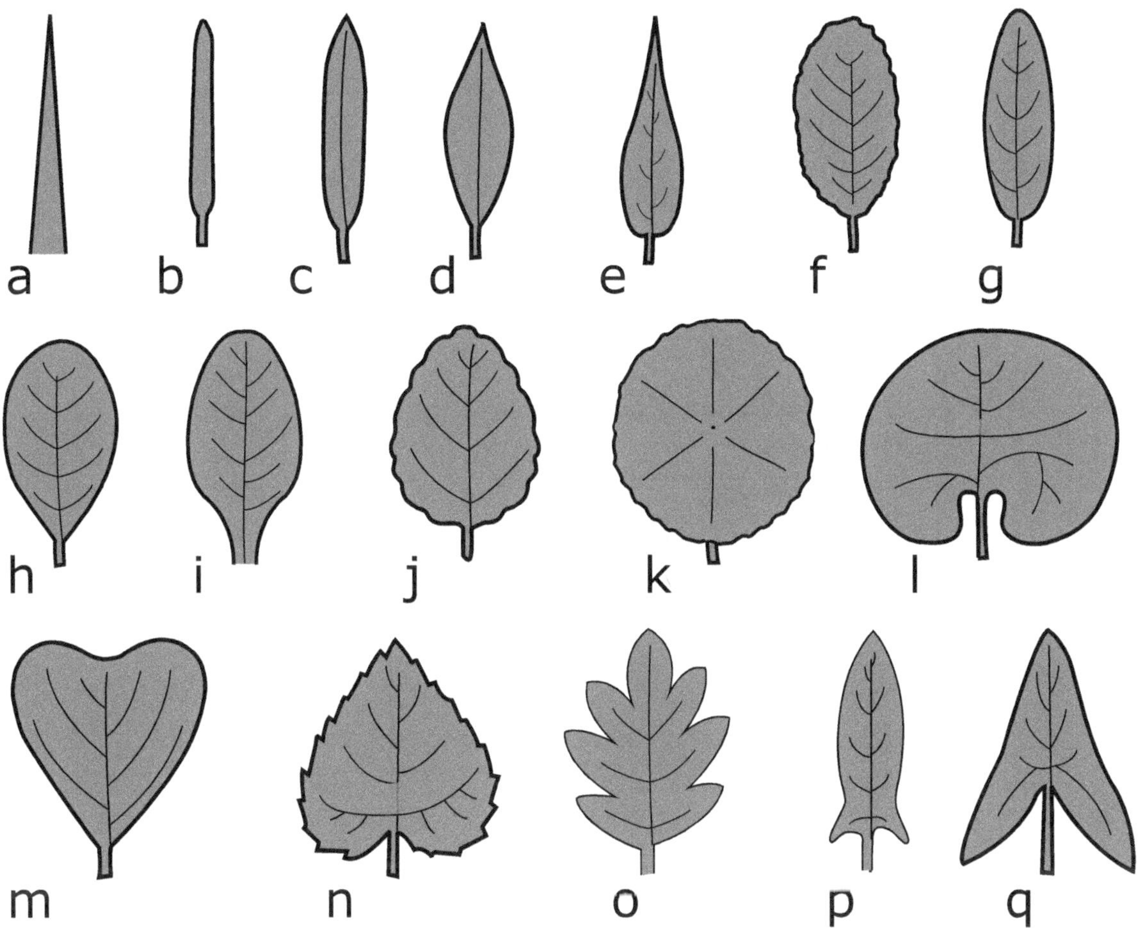

a. Acicular
b. Filiform
c. Linear
d. Elliptical
e. Lanceolate
f. Oval
g. Forget
h. Obovate
i. Cuneate
j. Ovate
k. Orbicular
l. Reniform
m. Obcordate
n. Battleship
o. Lobed
p. Hastada
q. Sagittarius

3.6. Flowers:

It is the organ through which plants can reproduce.

Tinzi

Tinzise' pari re'nisi awʉngwa'sʉya ni, ey awiri ʉnchwʉzari zoya'ba du kawa re'gʉwa ni.

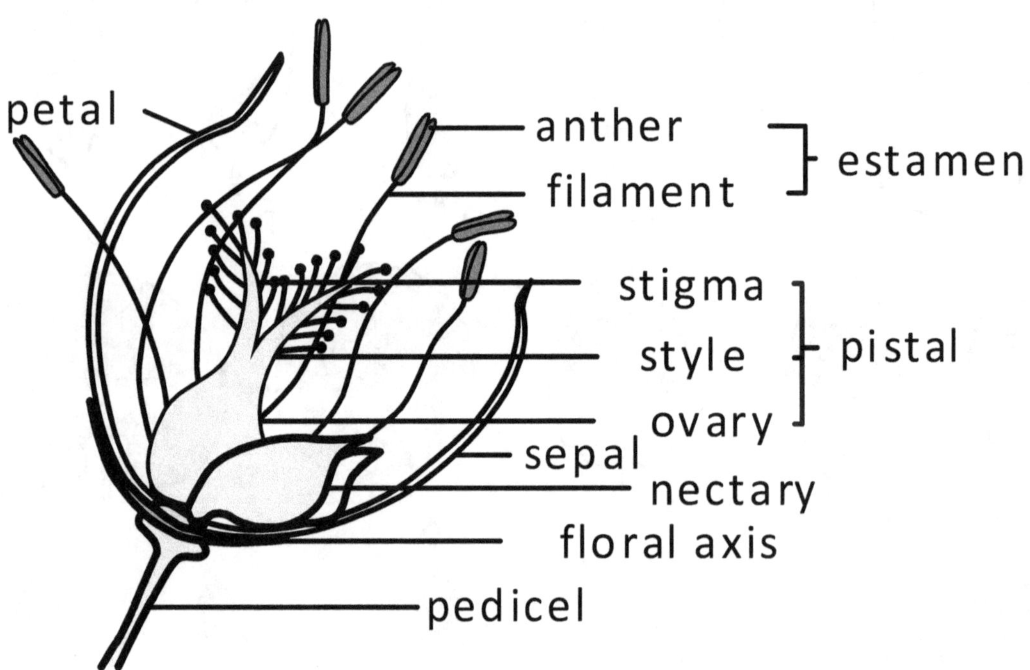

3.7. CLASSIFICATION AND IMPORTANCE OF PLANTS

Once the spiritual mother allowed the use the plants, these rights were assigned according to the needs of humankind and other living beings consuming plants.

Then the spiritual laws were known, as well as the tributes that should be made for the use of plants. According to this traditional law we can classify plants in six families:

1. EDIBLE PLANTS
2. PLANTS FOR CONSTRUCTION
3. PLANTS TO DYE
4. PLANTS FOR CEREMONIAL USE
5. MEDICINAL PLANTS
6. SACRED PLANTS

KɄN ɈUNA AZEY AZEY AWIRI A'MɄKANɄYAZEY NEYKA.

Kʉtʉkʉnʉn kingwi niwizakuse' kʉn ɉuna neykari a'mʉkanʉn gwa'sʉkwéy niwikʉre'gowna ni. Niwikʉɉuri ʉwa chwʉn nusi, awiri ana'nugase' ʉngey zoya anʉkʉɉwa'si niwikʉchukumana ni.

Ey unaɉu keywʉ kunsamʉ ʉnjwa'si nʉnnáɉuri tikʉrigʉn anizasari awkwey nanu' nanno. Emi ana'mʉkanʉyase' pari gunti.

Eyma kunsamʉse' pari azey azey tana wasaykwey niku'nanno, ʉyari chinwa re'nikwa na ni.

1. KɄN ɈUNA AGɄYA
2. KɄN ɈUNA INɄ BONɄYA
3. KɄN ɈUNA SI KɄKUMɄYA
4. KɄN ɈUNA MAMɄ SI A'MɄKANɄYA
5. KɄN ɈUNA WICHAMɄZEY
6. KɄN ɈUNA MAMɄ SI A'ZɄNA

3.7.1. EDIBLE PLANTS

Among the edible plants are those of common consumption and those of ceremonial consumption. However, none of these can be used without the prior permission of the "spiritual Mother". This law takes into account the seed before sowing it, the blessing of the harvest and the tribute after consumption.

KɄN ɈUNA AGɄYA

Kʉn ɉuna águya neykari ʉkín imʉ gey ukumʉya awiri ayeygwi mamʉ si ágʉya na ni. Ey anvwe'ki niwizákuse' ana'sisu' nari ʉngáktʉchʉ neki awkwey niwikʉná' neyka ni.

Niwi kunsamʉse'ri zaɉuna mamʉ sí izasana, ana'za unáɉuri ʉngánige' eygwi anizasana (kwadruse' i'ngwiri chwʉkwa ni).

Name Za'kinuga	Edible Part Gʉkwey Na'ba	Climate Inay Ʉwayke
Avocado Awakati	Fruit Agʉchʉ	Moderate Kʉmʉ Zʉnekʉ
Rice	Grain (Seeds) Ʉwa	Warm and Moderate Wiwi Awiri Kʉmʉ Zʉnekʉ
Auyama Ʉnmʉ	Fruit Agʉchʉ	Warm and Moderate Wiwi Awiri Kʉmʉ Zʉnekʉ
Sugar cane Kuñʉ	Stem Akʉnʉ	Warm and Moderate Wiwi Awiri Kʉmʉ Zʉnekʉ
Beans Ichʉ	Grain (Seeds) Ʉwa	Moderate Kʉmʉ Zʉnekʉ
Guineo Giñia	Fruit Agʉchʉ	Warm Wiwi Zʉna'ba
Lettuce Rechuga	Leaves Azachʉ	Moderate Kʉmʉ Zʉnekʉ
Corn In	Grain (Seeds) Ʉwa	Warm and Moderate Wiwi Awiri Kʉmʉ Zʉnekʉ
Malanga Maranga	Roots Akʉtʉ	Warm Wiwi Zʉna'ba
Mandarine Mandarina	Fruit Agʉchʉ	Warm Wiwi Zʉna'ba
Mango Mangu	Fruit Agʉchʉ	Warm and Moderate Wiwi Awiri Kʉmʉ Zʉnekʉ
Yam Ñame	Roots Akʉtʉ	Warm Wiwi Zʉna'ba
Orange Naranja	Fruit Agʉchʉ	Warm Wiwi Zʉna'ba
Wheat Trigu	Grain (Seeds) Ʉwa	Cold Kʉ zʉnargʉn
Yucca Irokwʉ	Roots Akʉtʉ	Warm Wiwi Zʉna'ba

EDIBLE PLANTS KʉN ɈUNA AGʉYA

3.7.2. CONSTRUCTION PLANTS

There are many plants that are used for construction, but there are traditional laws that regulate the use of them. In the same way, there are objects that can only be made by specific people as mandated by their spiritual law, for example: the tools for dyeing dresses and similar ones.

KʉN ɈUNA INʉ BONʉYA

Kʉn ɉuna inʉ gawkwéy neyka re'masi na ni, ey anʉwe'ki niwikunsámʉ rigʉndi tisʉn neki niwigwasu' na ni. Eymase' tá nari, mʉkʉ ʉnbonʉngwa, kʉ́rkʉna, karetia, nʉneykari ayey ikʉ mámʉse' kiaseynase' zʉ'n ʉwa ni.

Name	Part Used	Use in Construction	Where can be found?
Male Avocado	Stem Akʉnʉ	Houses, Puntaleras, Benches Urakʉ, gumʉkumʉyʉn, ákumʉya	Forrest Kʉ́nkʉnʉn
Anon	Cortex	Tie Houses Urakʉ-a'chunʉngwa	Great mountain
Bejuco	Stem Akʉnʉ	Harvest Maguey	Forrest
Calegallo	Whole akʉnʉ	Tie Houses Urakʉ-a'chunʉngwa	Everywhere
Cañaboba	Stem Akʉnʉ	Houses Urakʉ	
Carretillo	Stem Akʉnʉ	Houses, Puntaleras	Everywhere
Cedar	Stem Akʉnʉ	Wood, Houses	Mountain
Cha Granadillo	Stem Akʉnʉ	Bridges	Everywhere
Dina	Stem Akʉnʉ	Houses, Puntaleras	Forrest
Guaco	Stem Akʉnʉ	Houses, Puntaleras	Forrest
Guamo	Leaves Azachʉ	Puntaleras	Everywhere
Guava	Stem Akʉnʉ	Houses, Puntaleras, Benches	Forest hills
Higuito	Stem Akʉnʉ	Houses, Puntaleras	Everywhere
Iraka	Leaves Azachʉ	Houses	Everywhere
Kas Kʉnʉ	Stem Akʉnʉ	Houses, Puntaleras	Forrest
Kuracra	Stem Akʉnʉ	Houses, Tirantas	Mountain
Lacre	Stem Akʉnʉ	Houses, Puntaleras	Stubble

Name	Part Used	Use in Construction	Where can be found?
Laurel	Stem Akʉnʉ	Houses, Puntaleras	Small Mount
Macana	Stem Akʉnʉ	Puntaleras	Everywhere
Maguey	Leaves Azachʉ	Cords, Backpack	Stubble
Manzano Macho	Stem Akʉnʉ	Firewood, Puntaleras	Small Mount
Maquenque	Stem and Leaves Akʉnʉ awiri azachʉ	Haouses Urakʉ	Forrest
Palma	Stem and Bud Aʉnʉ awiri azachʉ	Houses, Brooms	Great mountain
Paraquito	Stem Akʉnʉ	Puntaleras	Great mountain
Samatia	Stem Akʉnʉ	Wood, Houses	Small Mount
Zula	Cortex and Stem	Houses	Everywhere

3.7.3. MEDICINAL PLANTS

There are varieties of healing plants, which are mostly for the exclusive use of the Mamo, but there are others that can be used by the "elders". As with all plants, proper tirbute must be made before using them.

KʉN ɈUNA WICHAMʉZEY

Kʉn ɉuna wichámʉzey diwʉ́n diwʉ́n kwey zoyaki nuga'ba pari mamʉ sí kinki umʉ́n a'mʉkánʉya chʉzʉna ni, ey ʉwe'ki umʉnte' a'zʉnase' ana'mʉkʉnasʉkweygwi apaw sikʉ izasana kinki awkwey nisiza ni.

Name	Part Used	Use	Where can be found?
Ajenjo	Leaves Azachʉ	Diarrhea Garia	Farms Cheykʉna
Cantameria	Leaves Azachʉ	Pimples Turinsa, atti	Everywhere Pinzʉnay
Chicoria	Roots Akʉttʉ	Diarrhea and Muscular aches Garia, gʉcha' me'neysʉkwa	Cold climate Kʉriwakʉ
Cola de Caballo	Everything Yowkʉchʉ	Waist Pain Gákʉnʉzánʉzey	Rivers and Puddles Ɉe meyna awiri tikʉnse'
Contra Gavilana	Leaves Azachʉ	Snake bite Gwiomʉ migʉkwa'ba	Everywhere Zʉnekʉ
Guaco	Bejuco Asía	Snake bite Gwiomʉ migʉkwa'ba	Mount, Stubble Kʉ́nkʉna awiri zachunse'
Guanábana	Leaves Azachʉ	Diarrhea Garia	Farms Cheykʉna
Guava	Leaves Azachʉ	Diarrhea Garia	Farms Cheykʉna
Hayo	Leaves Azachʉ	Wounds Mibeykumana'ba	Close to houses Urakʉ mʉcheygʉmʉ
Higuerón	Syrup Azʉjwa	Toothache Kʉkʉ zanʉ	Mount, Stubble
Lemon	Leaves and Fruit Azachʉ awiri agʉchʉ	Everything Pinna ɉuna wichamʉ	Farms Cheykʉna
Mejorana	Leaves Azachʉ	Diarrhea Garia	Puddles Tikʉn a'nikwʉyʉn
Orange	Bud Awmʉ	Everything Pinna ɉuna wichamʉ	Farms Cheykʉna

Name	Part Used	Use	Where can be found?
Ojo de Buey	Seeds Ʉwa	Snake bite Gwiomʉ migʉkwa’ba	Everywhere Zʉnekʉ
Paico	Everything Yowkʉchʉ	Waist Pain Gákʉnʉzánʉzey	Close to houses Urakʉ mʉcheygʉmʉ
Quinoa	Cortex Beykumana	Diarrhea Garia	Warm climate Wiwi zʉnárigʉn
Verbena	Stem and Leaves Akʉnʉ azachʉ	Colic Zun me’ko’kusʉyʉn	Farms Cheykʉna
Xanten	Leaves Azachʉ	Diarrhea Garia	Close to houses Urakʉ mʉcheygʉmʉ

3.7.4. PLANTS TO DYE

In order to use these, the material to be dyed is taken into account, that is, whether they are used in the manufacture of native elements, for use of the society in general, or for those materials that will be used in ceremonial activities; which will be colored with different dyes. All activities must be carried out in harmony with the laws of origin.

KɄN ɈUNA SI KɄKUMɄYA

Kʉn ɉuna si kʉkumʉngwazeyri ayeygwi a'mʉkanʉngwazeygwi ukumʉya. Inʉ zana nanʉndi emi tina'kʉchʉ mikʉnanʉngwazey nʉn, awi kéywʉri mamʉ sirigʉn gwi nʉn.

Ayeygwi kawi neki sikʉkumʉ na'no, diwʉ́n diwʉ́n sikʉkumʉyari a'mʉkanʉngwa'ba pari na ni, ʉyari ayéy kunsámʉse' a'nikwʉya name' (Kuaduru makeywase' chukwa ni).

Name	Part Used	Color	Material to be dyed
Batatia	Roots Akʉttʉ	Light yellow Chʉmi bosé kawi	Maguey Bechʉ
Cha' guayacan	Cortex Beykumana	Yellow Chʉmi	Maguey Bechʉ
Chʉ'nʉ	Roots or Cortex Akʉttʉ kwa beykumana	Yellow Chʉmi	Maguey Bechʉ
Contra Gavilana	Leaves or Cortex Azachʉ kwa beykumana	Light green Chʉkiruru bosé kawi	Maguey Bechʉ
Dina	Seeds Ʉwa'	Dark purple Moraw twé kawi	Maguey, Cotton Bechʉ, unkʉ
Diwidiwi	Seeds Zaɉuna	Light brown Ka'tin bosé	Maguey Bechʉ
Ga'dinwa	Leaves or Cortex Azachʉ awiri beykumana	Darn purple Moraw bosé kawi	Maguey, Cotton Bechʉ, unkʉ
Gujkʉna		Yellow Chʉmi	Maguey Bechʉ
Ɉeganʉ	Seeds Ʉwa'	Drak brown Ka'tin twé kawi	Cotton Unkʉ
Ɉwikʉnʉ	Leaves Azachʉ	Red Zi'i kawi	Cotton Unkʉ
Kasikwanʉ			
Ka'sira	Roots Akʉttʉ	Yellow Chʉmi	Maguey Bechʉ
Katimora	Seeds Ʉwa'	Opaque Red Aziti bosi kawi	
Kugwinʉ	Cortex beykumana	Brown Ka'tin	Maguey Bechʉ
Kʉnɉegwioma	Leaves or Cortex Azachʉ awiri beykumana	Yellow Chʉmi	
Kʉnsia Zinki	Roots Akʉttʉ	Dark yellow Achʉmi twé kawi	Maguey Bechʉ
Kʉnziti	Cortex Beykumana	Red Aziti	Maguey, Cotton Bechʉ, unkʉ
Kwanʉ	Roots Akʉttʉ	Yellow Achʉmi	Maguey Bechʉ

Name	Part Used	Color	Material to be dyed
Mʉnkwinʉ	Seeds and Cortex Azachʉ awiri beykumana	Yellow Achʉmi	Maguey Bechʉ
Murita	Stem Akʉnʉ	Yellow Achʉmi	Maguey Bechʉ
Nowra	Cortex Beykumana	Dark purple Ka'tin twé kawi	Maguey Bechʉ
Sibʉtuntu	Everything Yowkʉchʉ	Light grey Agu'guru	Maguey Bechʉ
Sikura	Leaves or Bejuco Azachʉ awiri asía	Black Twi kawi	Maguey, Cotton Bechʉ, unkʉ
Siwʉwʉ	Cortex Beykumana	Yellow Achʉmi	Maguey Bechʉ
Sizita	Leaves Azachʉ	Dark red Aziti twé kawi	Maguey, Cotton Bechʉ, unkʉ
Túmʉsi	Cortex Beykumana	Dark red Aziti twé kawi	Maguey Bechʉ
Urʉ	Leaves Azachʉ	Purple Moraw	Maguey, Cotton Bechʉ, unkʉ
Yarina	Leaves Azachʉ	Purple Moraw	Maguey Bechʉ

3.7.5. CEREMONIAL PLANTS

There are plants for exclusive use in religious activities, which can be used by the society in general, and are used according to activities of spiritual cleaning or spiritual tribute.

KʉN ɟUNA MAMʉ SIRIGʉN A'MʉKANʉYA

I'ngwi kʉn ɟuna kwʉyeykari mamʉ sí nikamʉ anikʉn nuge' a'mʉkanʉngwazey neyka ni, ʉyari pinna ikʉsin tikʉrigʉn anazasanʉngwa nari ey ukumʉya ni (Kwadru asewase' chwʉkwa ni).

Name	Part Used	Climate
Sibiano Siwianu	Stem Akʉnʉ	Warm Wiwi zʉnekʉ
Frailejon Punʉ	Leaves Azachʉ	Cold Kʉ zʉnargʉn
Calabaza Poporo	Calabazo So	Mild Kʉ zʉna cheyna
Wet weather Frailejon Tiɟo'nʉ	Leaves Azachʉ	Cold Kʉ zʉnargʉn
Ayu Jayu	Leaves Azachʉ	Mild Kʉ zʉna cheyna
Corn In	Leaves Azachʉ	Mild Kʉ zʉna cheyna
Umʉtiki	Seeds Zaɟuna	Mild Kʉ zʉna cheyna
Cutting grass Zi'zi	Seeds Zaɟuna	All Pinzʉnay
River Frailejon ɟepunʉ	Leaves Azachʉ	Mild Kʉ zʉna cheyna

3.7.6. SACRED PLANTS

The law of origin determines that, when a plant is born in a sacred place, it has the same value as the sacred place and therefore, tribute shall be made. Such plants can't be cut for any reason.

KʉN ɈUNA MAMʉ Si' A'ZʉNA

Kunsamʉ kʉtʉkʉnʉn zanʉ ye'ri: "kʉn ka'gʉ́mʉse" a'zʉna'ba bonʉye'ri ayeygwi akingwi a'zari a'mesi zoya ni. Ey ʉwame'beysʉ wi'na na ni.

3.7.7. CONSERVATION OF PLANTS

For the conservation of the plants, everything established in the law of origin must be complied with, each plant must be cleaned before used and the necessary tributes to the Mother shall be made, so everything will remain in balance.

KʉN CHWI AWKWEYKA

Kʉn chwi awkweykari kunsamʉ sí yow a'nikwʉya ʉnchunhamʉ kawa na' no; tikʉrigʉn izasari, azey azey Ikʉ ɉuna kwʉyeyka a'mʉkanʉngwa'sʉn ʉnye'ri, azaku sikʉ sari awkwa ni, ʉyari, ʉyéy zaku Ɉinase' chusanáy ʉnchuney nanʉn chwʉn nuga, ikwʉn nuga kau' nanunno. Umʉ́n ínʉki kwʉyeykari kʉchonu'nanʉn gwasi.

3.8. PEDAGOGICAL ACTIVITIES

Perform the following activities and complement your knowledge about plants.

1. Make an image of plants with all their parts, color them, then cut them into squares, and reconstruct as if it were a puzzle.

2. Mention other plants that you know and were not mentioned in this Chapter.

3. Write two paragraphs discussing the use of plants in your home.

4. Choose the correct answer: The plants live in:

a. In water
b. In the sky
c. In water and land
d. In the air

NIKAMʉ

Ema nikamʉ awa unáyuri kunsamʉ kawʉnka'sa awkwa.

1. Dibuju du kawi ʉnnusi pinna kʉnari gow unáyuri ʉnbey awiri ʉncho'sukwey kwi awkwa.

2. In'geygwi kʉn ɟuna ma nʉɟwa'sʉya be neki nʉchu'gwi neyka wasey awkwa.

3. Mowga re'nikwa nánʉkin mikeynakʉ kʉn ʉnka'mʉkʉnhakumey zoyeyka a'sa awkwa.

4. In'gwi taneyka a'guka awkwa:
   Kʉn ɟuna bekʉ kuya nanno.
   a. Ɉese'
   b. Ku'nawa
   c. Ɉese' awiri ka'se'
   d. Buntikʉnʉse'.

4. ANIMALS

4.1. GENERAL GOALS

Reaffirm the need to conserve the habitat of animals and prevent them from becoming extinct.

Promote that students value, respect and use animals appropriately, taking into account both traditional Iku laws and Western concepts.

Visualize the classification of animals according to their habitat, their characteristics and their use.

Know a part of our traditional history and its reference to animal species through reading assignments and open discussions.

ANA'NUGA ɈINA

EYMEY KʉZARI A'KUMANA NI IZANʉNGW A NEYKA

Umʉ́n kinki, gʉmʉsinʉ ɉinase'ri, pinna aná'nuga azey azey kwʉyeykari chwi, wa'misu' nari rizweingwa neyka kʉyʉn kinki nusi, ʉyari tikumey neki zwei' nanʉngwasi.

Gʉmʉsinʉ riwiwya ɉinari pinna aná'nuga ɉina agákʉchʉ ʉwa neyka kwa mamʉ sírigʉn zʉ'n kʉɉúnʉye' gʉkwey nigari 1 chwi kinki zweykwa key kumʉ ka' si ukumʉngwasi.

Winde'riwiwya ɉinari pinna aná'nuga kwey ʉwa neykari chwi, chow a'chwi, a'mʉkʉna na' no ʉwari niwizákuse' niwikʉchusaneykari uzwey nanno.

Aná'nuga kwey ʉwa neykari, áykʉnʉ áykʉnʉ kwʉya'ba se kʉnari, bémey kawi kʉriwiwkwa nanʉndi uyari ʉyéy kinki kawi, bema a'mʉkʉna nanʉndi ʉyari ʉya ni ʉwari; niwi kunsamʉ si zanʉ awiri bunachʉ sí zanʉ dikin ɉwa'si
awiri, niwi enʉnáy nari ʉnkʉriwin niwingwasi. Niwikunsamʉrigʉndi du kinki se kʉnari umʉnte' a'zʉna ɉina a'zasisi, pinna aná'nuga ɉuna kwákumey ʉwa neyka riwi, paperi a'kumey una neyka ya awagwi unáɉuri yow umʉ́n agʉnkwʉyá neykari, nʉkʉyʉn kein du na' nanno.

4.2. ORIGIN OF ANIMALS (Reading Assignment)

GʉMʉSINʉ AWIWKWA'BA SEKʉNANʉKWA

As we saw earlier, the mythology of the Iku people (a.k.a. Arhuacos), teaches that, at the beginning of the material existence of living beings, only humans were known.

Then the "Mother", according to the needs that arose, was transforming nature into plants and much later into animals.

When the "Mother" had established the laws for the proper use and conservation of plants, she noted that other fundamental elements were needed. Many years had passed and people had adapted to the coexistence and harmony with plants.

Yow nʉkin gʉmʉsinʉ anʉkʉyʉngwa mika'nisi anʉwiʉngwa nʉnnige'ri, gʉmʉsinʉ awiyari ema paperi yow nʉkin yʉkwa kʉnisi zwey nanno. Ey unige'ri in'gweti in'gweti keykumʉngwa neykari umʉ́n ʉyari nʉnaí kinki kawi ʉnchunhey zweingwasi. Ingʉri azi nari kʉchʉ ʉwari, azi kawi gʉmʉsinʉ kéykumey wazwein nu'na nandi, ʉyari diw-fln re'gau' nari ʉyey kinki ingʉri ʉnnusí azwein du na' nanno, ey anúnige' yow niwe' zʉnneykari ingiti kindi niwikʉnchori zoriza ni. Ema niwikʉnchori zoriza neykari riwiwya ɉinari ʉyari aguzanikʉn kinki gwa'si, azi neykari ey agwakunno a'zanun gwa'si, awiri agawin nu'nige'ri du kawi re'takʉn gwa'sʉn gwʉn

All family members had their farms were organized, but some still spent their nights collecting edible fruits, which was not part of the law of origin. (traditional law)

ʉnkʉriwikweykari du kawi ʉnka'ɟu nánʉko.

Gʉmʉsinʉ anʉgawí ʉnzoya'bari, ʉya nikamʉ kʉnʉneykari ga'kʉnámʉri ano'kukwéy zʉneyka í, zoyʉn du na'nanno, awiri ʉndigawiyeykari bemeyki neki nisiri agano'kwa awʉngwa neyka re'tasi zwein du nariza ni; ʉyari riwiwya ɟina wina'zanʉkwʉyʉkin gwi uzori au' nanno. Akowna neykari ikʉ awiwya, ema kinki gʉmʉsínʉse' kuwʉsʉngwa neyka awiri riwiwya ɟina neykari umʉnte a'zuna ɟina amipáw ɟinase', mámʉse' neykari ey kinki a'zasisi uzweíngwa a'chwi zweykwa, ey anu'nige'ri ʉnkʉrigawin nugari umʉ́n kinki ɟuma'kumey wazwemgwasi.

After some time, the "Mother" appeared to do justice, punishing these individuals; giving them other duties and rights. These were converted into edible animals, some of common consumption and others of

KɄTɄKɄNɄN ANA'NUGA KWAKUMEY UYE

Kʉtʉkʉnʉn ínʉki chwʉzari awʉngwa neyka wintukwase'ri ikʉ nʉkin kwʉya nʉnna; ey awi zákuse' kʉɟunin ʉwari kʉn ɟuna chwʉzanisi zoyana, awi zʉnnáriri aná'nuga chwʉzanisi zweinpʉnna.

unique and exclusive consumption in religious activities.

Aná'nuga du ʉ́nkʉchwi, zi azu' nari uzweykwa ní guga, zákuse' kwasa awaki nuse'ri, ɟwa umʉn a'zʉna neyka anʉme'nusi zweykwazey niwikʉjuna awnʉnno azʉnna.

After many more years, the "Mother" noted that many gunamu (members) of other communities, showed greater interest and concern for home-related activities, or serve as partners to the owners of things, so the ''Mother" determined that they would be animals called "friends of the home"(pets). These animals were considered friends of the home, and therefore, it was forbidden to eat them.

Birin ʉnzanika uye'ri kʉn ɟunasin re'nokwamʉ, uzoyamʉ ikʉse'ri ʉnkʉriwia winowna; ey awi ʉya kingwi ʉnkwazwein nuga na'nʉnno.

More time passed by and, children grew up showing some determination and willingness to serve when they were needed in tragic or difficult times, when people needed to immediately move a sick person to distant places, or when sacred materials

Ikʉ winnʉnari in'gweti chey du zari winʉkʉna nʉnna ʉweki ʉɟwari in'gwizey chey nʉnekʉ zagʉn zoya nʉnna ey awi ʉnzanika uye'ri zaku du zakusi nase'ri, zágʉya ɟinari aná'nuga re' gow awi, mamʉ chwi agʉngwa, awiri binzari neki

were needed from other regions, etc. Then these were called by the "Mother" to be part of the sacred animals and some to serve as a means of transportation.

During those times, life was more pure, everyday activities were more linked to the spiritual growth of people, in the same way ceremonial tasks were more widespread, so more ritual elements and materials were used.

agʉ́'kʉchʉ awʉngwa nari re'gowna.

Eygwi zanika uye, zákuri gunamʉ ʉɟwun ʉɟwun zanʉ urákʉse' ukumʉya neyka umʉ́m agʉzari zwein pʉnna; ey ʉwame zakuse'ri urakʉse' ukumʉya zʉɟwʉ́nʉkʉnʉ nanʉngwa nari re'gowna.

Ʉyari, aná'nuga urákʉse' niwika'mʉkʉna, agu'neyka ey awga na'nʉnno.

Umʉ́n birin zanika awi, eygwi nare'ri, gʉmʉsinʉ kwákumey zweínpana ikʉnari beki mʉnʉ rinuzweykwa nʉna'ba, kwa a'buru aɟwʉn zanʉ mikʉɟuri awkwa nʉna'bari ikʉnase' ɟwirí winawa a'ɟunana; ey awi zákuse' ke' ʉwʉn uye'ri ʉyéy nanʉngwa a'mʉkʉna, a'zʉna, zagósʉya nanʉngwa amasáy re'gowna na ni.

One day, while the Mamo were in congregation, they analyzed that, for the success of their activities, entrusted by the "Mother", some people would have to participate as a means of information, which would be responsible for communicating to the Mamo any act of irregularity committed by members of any family or any other case of interest. Then these people were called by the "Mother" and were transformed into messenger animals.

Finally, some people were born with great concern about other individuals and the social well-being of people, both in a material and spiritual way, so they were converted into life-saving animals and to be used in ceremonial acts, especially those related to the health of living beings.

The "Mother" established spiritual laws that make us equal to other living beings in nature, but humans must ensure the conservation of all the natural beings and the environment, which he uses on a daily basis.

Eyméy nari zwein nuse 'ri niwikunuku nari akwey azoyana~ ínʉki umʉn ɉumʉ a 'nisi nari mámʉsin rimasáy ɉwa ʉnbori zoya'ba a'buru si nenʉn umʉ́n ʉnkʉriwí zweykwey niga ni.

I'mʉ́nʉri mamʉ ɉina rinre'takʉn nusi zákuse' ʉnchunhey zweykwa gwasi niwikʉchusana ʉwanʉndi in'gwi ʉɉwa ga'niwikéy awʉngwa áykʉnʉ ʉnka'guka awamʉ kawnanno wina'zʉnna; ey awi zaku ʉnka'zasisi nare'ri, ʉyéy ʉnchori
aná'nuga ga' yʉngwa nari zákuse' re'gowna ni.

A'kowna neykari; pinna kwey niwinmi'naki nuga in'gwi akwey ʉwa awiri nʉn nenʉn du gunti kʉzari akwey zweingwa a'zʉneyka kwakumey zoyana ni.

Ʉnchunhey zweykwa gwasi zákuse' niwikʉchusanari: niwinmi 'naki nugasin eyma umʉ́n azʉna na 'no.

Zaka'chó'sʉkwey nanu' neyka niwikʉchukumana ni, ʉwame' yow kwey ʉwari ʉ́nkʉchwi kʉchó'nanu'kwa niwezari sigin ʉnka'mʉkanʉkwéy neykasin i'ngwi ʉnkʉchwamʉ gunti niwikawa mamʉse'ri eyméy gwasi wásʉyani.

4.3. IMPORTANCE OF ANIMALS

Taking into account what is established in the traditional law, we can say that no living being can remain isolated, because in order to live, we are forced to live together and serve each other. For this reason, animals play an important role in everyone's life.

Animals not only serve to improve the traditional food diet, but also strengthen our spiritual growth. Others serve us as a means of transportation, some are means of information to the Mamo and the elderly, while others fulfill the function of caring for and protecting the lives of human beings, animals and nature in general.

ANA'NUGARI A' MʉKARI WINKWʉYA NI

Kwamʉ warunhʉn nusi nanʉndi, bema neki emi ka'gʉmʉ tina kwʉyeykari áykʉnʉ kwʉkwey neki aniwikʉnanu' na' nanno. Emi kwaweri meza'nʉndi azi ne nanʉnki i'ba kinki kwʉkwey niwikʉna'no. i'ba ʉnka'mʉkari, rinahchwi zoyamʉ kau' no. Ey ʉwame' aná'nuga neykari peykʉ ikʉ ka'mʉkanʉn nuga na' nanno.

Aná'nuga winneykari zamʉ sí nʉkin a'mʉkánʉya neki na' nanʉnno. Emi manʉnka inaykwa'ba, arunʉnkwa'ba, jʉmu mékʉsi mika'mukánʉkwa ni. Iwa in'gwi peykʉ neki zweingwasi, ga'kʉnamʉ mámʉse' kwa sakúkʉse' neki kuzweingwasi.

4.4. CLASSIFICATION OF TRADITIONAL ANIMALS

According to traditional laws, we find three groups of animals, which are among the laws managed by the Mamo and in the activities entrusted to him. However, the same law allows us to make other subdivisions, taking into account the uses given to the animals, either by the society in general, or in events linked to individual or social spirituality.

Taking into account the environment where they live (the habitat), we can consider three groups of animals: aquatic, terrestrial and aerials (flying).

ANA'NUGA ɈUNA MAMɄRIGɄN ZAKA'NUGA

Niwikunsamʉ siri maykʉnʉ ɉuna nánʉkin ana'nuga kwʉya ni, ʉya ɉinari in'gwiri nʉkin mámʉse' zʉ'n ga'kʉnamʉ kʉɉwá'sʉya ni, iwa in'gwiri kunsámʉse' kingwi diwʉ́n awi a'mʉkanʉngwa'sʉkwéy yeyka ni, ey ʉwe'ri ʉya'bari re'masi nari kwa use' zʉ'n mamʉrigʉndi gwakʉkwnéy niga ni.

4.4.1. AQUATIC ANIMALS

They are responsible for transporting the materials used in spiritual cleanings and tributes by the Mamo and their gunamu (community members), and which have been transported to the oceans, where the spiritual "Mother" is located and ready to receive all the negative things.

ANA'NUGA JESE' KWUYEYKA

Ema aná'nugari powruse' a'buru ani'na neyka mʉkuriwa sikʉ uzweingwasi (zaku) gʉnsinna; ɨina ipanʉngwanari uzoya ni. Ey awʉndi ʉyeygwi semaneru zana' a'mʉkʉna na'no.

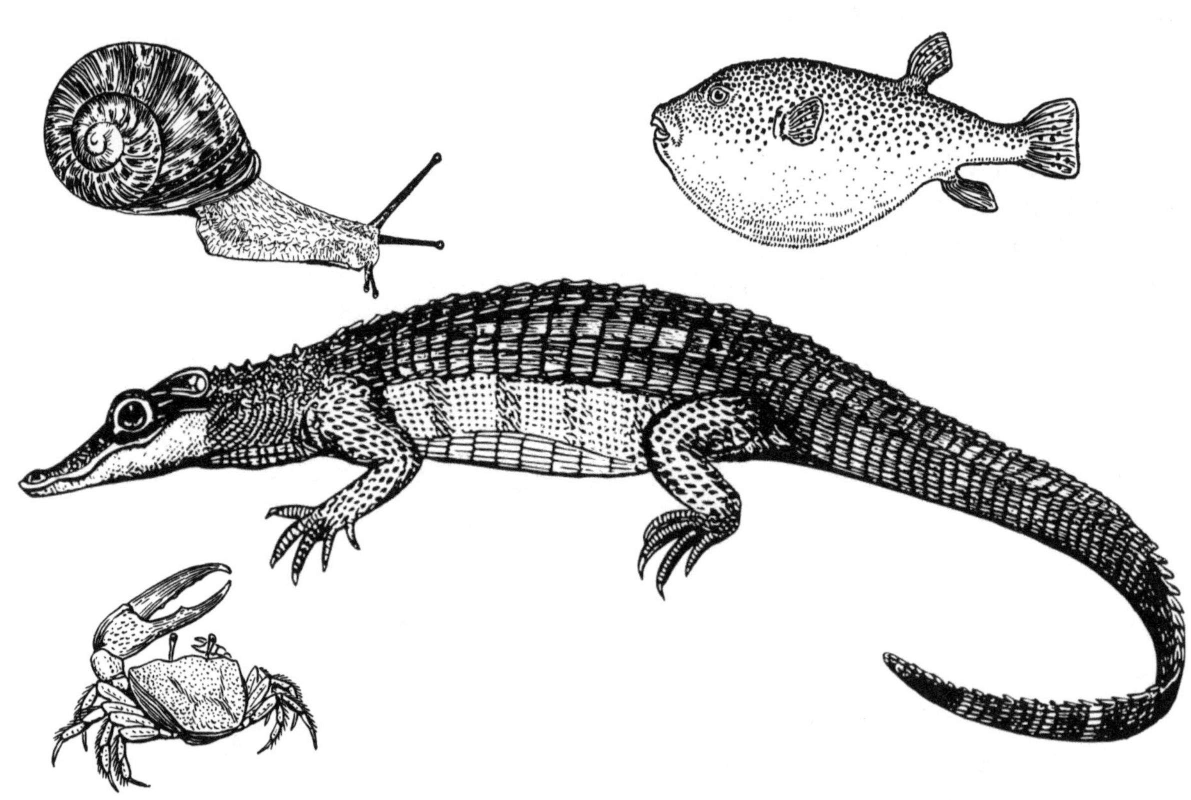

These animals include,

Guabino
River crab
Trout
Seashell
Alligator

Ema ana'nuga neykari ema ni:

Ucho'
Uti
Wakʉ
Urumʉ ɨiwʉse' zanʉ
Caimán

4.4.2. LAND ANIMALS

These were chosen by the "Mother" to contribute to the activities entrusted to the Mamo and related to the material and spiritual development, both in the individual and the social life of people, and of every being that inhabits the universe.

Meaning those animals related to the well-being of people, and in mandatory compliance of the traditional laws, to ensure the balance and conservation of the natural resources.

ANA'NUGA KA'SE' WINKUYA

Ema amá'nuga ɨinari zákuse' ingʉ diwʉ́n nari a'mʉkanʉngwasi chusanari, ʉya ɨinari mamʉ sí nikamʉ kwánige, ey awi keywʉri emi tina' nariri tikʉrigʉn zagunamʉsʉngwasi chukumana ni; re'masi nari kwa in'gweti ikʉ nʉnkura'ba. Ey ʉwame' azi nanʉnki ikʉri aná'nugase' párigwi kwʉkwey niwikʉniku' no, ey awiri, emi ínʉki kwʉyeyka chwi, ikwey awkwari ʉya'ba pari gunti uzweykwéy niku' no.

Eyméy ʉwa'ba pari kunsamu a'nikwʉyáy achunamʉ kau' nanno, pinna ɨuna kwʉyeykari i'ngwi dikin nari zweinntwmgwasi, be, zakuse'ri ʉyéy kunsamʉ chusana gun nandi.

These animals include,

Ñeque
Chipmunk
Dogs
Tigrillo
Sheep

Ana'nuga ey awgari ema ni:

Asareku
Kwi'ɨumaka
Perʉ
Seykunuma
Weja

4.4.3. AERIAL ANIMALS (BIRDS)

These are responsible for transporting or carrying the materials used in spiritual tributes, spiritual cleanings and everything related to the good things that are done to feed the spirit. Such materials are taken to Father Kaku Bunkwákukwi.

ANA'NUGA DRÚNʉYA ɈINA

Ema aná'nuga ɉinari ánugwe duna neyka a'buru bónʉye' winʉkuzori a'rimʉkʉna ni.

Ema ánugwe dunari niwikakʉ Bunkwakukwi sikʉ winʉkuzoya ni.

These animals include pigeons and other common birds.

Ema ana'nuga ɉinari sisío ɉina dururí ʉwa ɉina neyka ni.

Additionally, people could make their own classification of animals, but in reality, for the Iku culture only those established by the law of origin count.

Ikʉri áykʉnʉ ingʉ diwʉn nari aná'guga re'basʉkwéy kʉnʉna ní, ey ʉwe'ki kunsámʉse' a'nikwʉyáy zʉ'n wazoya ni. Sanusi zaka' cho'kumana nungwari mamʉrigʉn zaka'nugay na' no.

Without forgetting the laws previously noted on aquatic, terrestrial and aerial animals, we could make the following subdivision:

- EDIBLE ANIMALS
- TRANSPORTATION ANIMALS
- SACRED ANIMALS

Eyma'ba pari chwʉn nusi nandi eygwi re'basʉkwéy na' nʉnno, agʉyeyka, mina'mékʉkwa awiri mamʉ sí a'mʉkʉna warunʉndi:

- ANA'NUGA ÁGʉYA
- ANA'NUGA A'ZAGOKUMʉYEYKA
- ANA'NUGA MAMʉ SI ɈWAKAWʉ NEYKA

4.4.4. EDIBLE ANIMALS

4.4.4.1. - COMMON CONSUMPTION

They are those that the traditional law allows to eat by all the members of the family, in any daily activity, but in previous harmony with the mother. These animals include cows, sheep, pigs, chickens, turkeys, and the like.

ANA'NUGA ÁGʉYA

- PINNASE' ÁGʉYA

Ema ɉinari umʉ́n pinnase' neki gʉkwéy nari zákuse' chusana na ni, binzari kwa ínʉki neki awʉn nusi, ey ʉwe'ki apáw síkʉri izasanamʉ kinki kawa ni.

4.4.4.2. – ANIMALS OF CEREMONIAL CONSUMPTION

They are those used in ceremonial events and are provide special nutrients for the growth of the spirit. These are often used in the baptism of children, in the preparation of a Mamo, or in the blessing of large buildings. These animals include iguanas, cocks, squirrels, pooches and small birds.

- ANA'NUGA MAMɄRIGɄN ANE' AGɄYA

Ema aná'nuga ɉinari nʉkin mamʉ sí ananʉn nuge' ágʉya ni ánugwe ɉumʉ kʉsʉngwasi, zizi ɉwa kʉkumʉye', mamʉ sí rigawiye', urakʉ ɉwa kʉkumʉye; eyméy nari zʉ'n ágʉya ni.

4.4.5. TRANSPORTATION ANIMALS

Although the "Mother" initially assigned transportation or cargo animals to be used in difficult tasks, some of these animals currently perform other functions. And, the animals that today serve as a means of transportation, were primarily brought by the western man or Bunachu.

Some of these transportation animals include: donkeys, mules, horses, and oxes, among others.

ANA'NUGA A'ZAGOKUMɄYEYKA

Kʉtʉkʉnʉn kingwi íkʉri ana'nuga ʉnka'zagosʉkwazey nari zakuse'ri kʉchusana. Iniki mʉ a'zʉna ʉnkʉgosʉngwasi winʉkʉchusane 'ki iwari ingʉ diwʉ́n nari a'mʉkari kwʉya ni.

Aná'nuga iwa íkʉse'ʉnka'zagósʉya bekʉ neki uzoya kwʉyeykari bunáchʉse' una'na gunti neyka ni; ʉya neykari: Buru, machu kʉgowro, buey, mura, gunti neyka ni.

4.4.6. SACRED ANIMALES

Sacred animals are those that the traditional law prohibits to eat, and have been chosen by the "Mother" as elements that contribute to the success of the activities entrusted to the Mamo. According to this law we can classify them in two cathegories:

ANA'NUGA ɈWAKAWɄ NEYKA

Ema aná'nuga ɉinari e' kʉtʉkʉnʉn kingwi niwipawse' ayéy tikʉrigʉn tina mámʉse' ka'mʉkanʉngwazey nari chukumaname' gʉwi'na na ni. Eymi warunʉn nusi mowga ɉuna na ni.

4.4.6.1. - MESSENGERS

These are those animals responsible for keeping the Mamo and elders at notice of things that happen or can happen. These animals include the owl, parrot, nightingale, kwiwi (night bird) and jo'kwinsiro (bird's name)

- ANA'NUGA GA' YEYKA

Ema aná'nuga tanari mamʉ ywi riwanʉn gwa'sʉya ey awga ni awiri zanʉngweykasi umʉn ga' yeyka ni ʉya tanari. Ɉo'kwinsiro in'gwi na' nʉnno.

4.4.6.2. – OF CEREMONIAL USE

These animals have the function of saving lives. They are sacrificed and used as elements for spiritual tasks related to the health of people and the well-being of nature; such is the case with spiders, scorpions and beetles.

- ANA'NUGA MAMɄRIGɄN KɄɈUNɄYA

Ʉyari aná'nuga minagukʉkweyka ey awga ni, kʉɉuna ʉweri gwaka awi a'buru re'bónʉya ni, du niwezanʉngwa nari i'ngwi yow niwinmi'naki nugasin nenʉ́n.

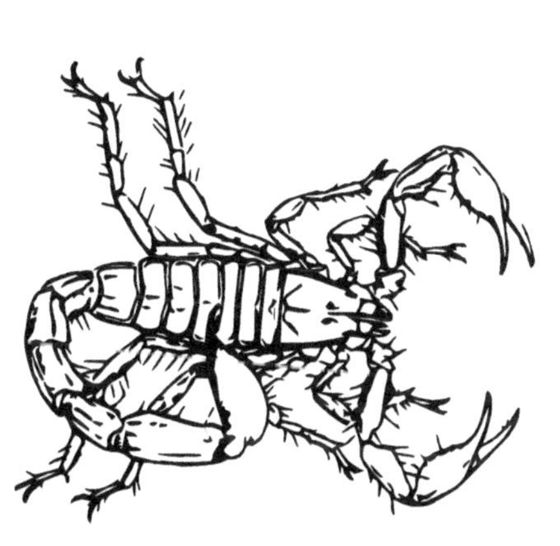

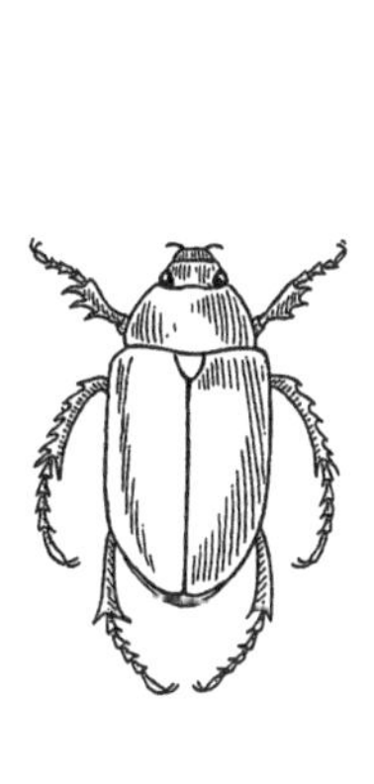

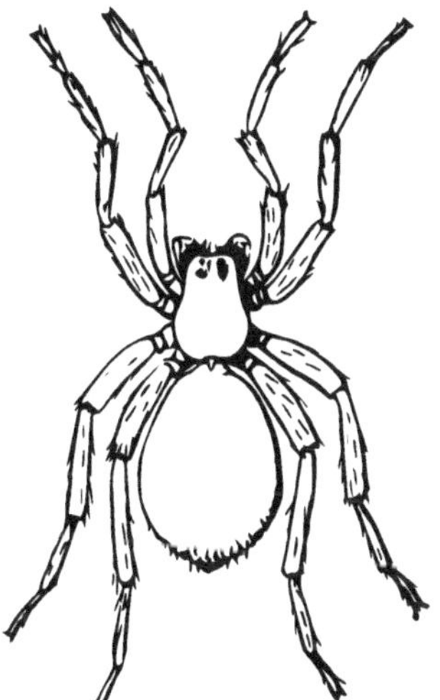

4.5. PEDAGOGICAL ACTIVITIES:

Classify animals according to their habitat.

NIKAMʉ

Emi ana'nuga chwʉzʉneykari azey azey kwʉyeyka chwʉzʉnhasa awkwa.

4.6. CONSERVATION OF ANIMALS

For the conservation of animals, it is the Iku's duty to pay tribute or spiritual offerings. For example, making tributes to the Mother, and thank her for all animals, as established in the Law of Origin, or to ask her for guidance on preventing animals from becoming extinct, and thus promoting balance among all beings of nature.

ANA'NUGA ʉNKʉCHWI ZWEYKWEYKA

Aná'nuga tana kʉcho'nánʉkwa ʉwari gunti chwamu niwikau' nanno anugwekin nari ka'pinsi, izasari, zákuse' ipʉnasʉn gun ase' kʉtʉkʉnʉn gwana'ba ta uzori kʉcho'ná'kwa a'chwi dikin riwari rinhuzwey nánʉko.

4.7. ANIMALS — ANA'NUGA ꞲINA

AQUATIC ANIMALS	ANA'NUGA JESE' KWUYEYKA
Guabino	Kʉneyru
River crab	Uti
Trout	Wakʉ
Seashell	Ꞁo'tinwʉ
Alligator	Kayman

LAND ANIMALS	ANA'NUGA KA'TINA RI KWʉYA
Ñeque	Asareku
Chipmunk	Kwi'ɟumaka
Birds	Sisio
Dog	Perʉ
Tigrillo	Tigriyu

EDIBLE ANIMALS	ANA'NUGA AGUYA
COMMON CONSUMPTION	**PINNASE' AGUYA**
Cow	Sʉna'gekuya
Sheep	Weja
Pork	Chinu
Chicken	Keyna
Turkey	Piku

EDIBLE ANIMALS	ANA'NUGA GA'ʉNBORI
TRADITIONAL CONSUMPTION	**ÁGʉYA**
Chipmunk	Kwi'ɟumaka
Mutt	Zinki
Monte Birds	Dirunʉya Kʉnkʉnʉn Zanʉ
Iguana	Iwanʉ
Guartinaja	Otiki

TRANSPORTATION ANIMALS	ANA'NUGA A'ZAGOKUMʉYEYKA
Mule	Mura
Donkey	Buru
Ox	Buey
Horse	kʉgowro
SACRED ANIMALS	**ANA'NUGA ɈWAKAWʉ NEYKA**
CEREMONIAL USE	**ANA'NUGA MAMʉRIGʉN KʉɈUNʉYA**
Spider	Mʉnkwʉ
Cucarrones	Tiwi,
Scorpion	Zeyku
Beetle	Gadío
SACRED ANIMALS	**ANA'NUGA ɈWAKAWʉ NEYKA**
MESSENGERS	**ANA'NUGA GA' YEYKA**
Jo'kwinsiro	Ɉo'kwinsiro
Owl	Bunku
Parrot	Kwiromʉ
Mockingbird	Chʉ́mʉsi
Night bird	Kwiwi

4.8. PEDAGOGICAL ACTIVITIES:

1. . Which animals are used as spiritual tribute materials?

2. What is the benefit provided by crabs in spiritual tributes?

NIKAMʉ

1. Bema nanno ana'nuga a'buru re'bónʉya.

2. Utiri be na'ba a'mʉkánʉya no.

THE SOIL AND ROCKS

5. THE SOIL

5.1. GENERAL GOALS

Highlight the soil relevance to all living beings.

Recognize the sacred value that the land has for the Iku.

Identify some of the sacred sites that are part of the Iku territory.

RE'NIKWɄYA IN'GWI: KA'

EMEY KɄJZARI A'KUMANA NI IZANUNGWA NEYKA

Ka'se' chʉká a'zʉna ɉina winkwey ʉwa neyka winamʉkánʉya chow a'chwʉn gwa'si.

Ka'gʉmʉ íkʉse' zakʉkanugáy kʉnari ɉwa'sa awi chow a'chwi zweingwasi, niwika' gʉ́mʉsé, mukuy.

Mʉrundwa, gwiáchʉnʉ kwímʉkʉnʉ niwi ka'gʉmʉse' kwʉyeyka ɉwa' sa awʉngwasi.

5.2. CONCEPT OF SOIL/GROUND

From the spiritual point of view, the ground/soil is considered our Mother. The soil is the experience, the base, the foundation that all beings occupy since creation.

Seeds of all kinds, and necessary for our existence, find their home in the soil.

It is also the place of harvest and other activities, both for common use and ceremonial events.

KA' ɈWA'SAMʉ

Niwi ikʉ nʉnkureykari ánugwe siri, Niwizaku zana nanunanno ka' kwey ʉwa neyka, ʉya'ba kwa kwákumey zʉnáy ayéy a'bori winkwey, diwʉ́m diwʉ́m chʉká a'zʉna ɉina kwey, nanʉngwa nari Ey ma ɉuna chʉwi nika awʉngwa name', niwi ka'mʉkanʉngwa nari, kagʉ́mʉse' ayéy ʉnchunhey ʉnzasari eymeygwi nisi zoya name' a'nikuyáy ʉnchunhey kʉnsamʉ sí.

5.3. SOIL/GROUND/LAND USES

The soil/ground/land is useful to all living beings.

According to the traditional law, Mother Earth was created to take care of the soil and land. The conservation of the soil is done through payment of spiritual tribute by all human beings. In the Iku land, they work together and cultivate for the

A'MʉKÁNʉYA

ʉyéy a'mʉkana awizʉneyka, ka'se' kwey ʉwa neyka, achuney emi niwi ka'mukana awiza nanʉnno.

Ka'gʉmʉ, kinki ʉyéy ʉnkʉnchunhey awkwa name' nanu' nari, ema mamʉ sirigʉn ʉyey ʉnchʉney zori ínʉki achuney neki nanu' nari. Ema ánugwe si izasari zoya na' nanno.

common benefit. They farm cassava, malanga, guineo, potato, corn, onion, ayu or hayo, and many others crops. The land also serves for animal husbandry and humans were assigned to those tasks. However, in order to make proper use of the land, the Iku must first make spiritual offerings and pay tribute to the Mother land, so balance with the universe is maintained.

Ʉmʉnʉkʉnʉse' ri niwi ikʉ nʉnkureykari ka' gʉmʉse' zamʉ ɉuna niwi ka'mʉkʉna ʉnzarisi ʉwa ni, Irokwʉ, giñia, maranga, trumʉ, ín, siboya, ayu, awiri pinna ɉuna. Ey awiri ka'gʉmʉri ána'nuga ʉnkicho' si niwi azweingwazey nari a'mʉkanʉngwasi. Ey ʉwe'ki níwiri, mika'mʉkanʉngwasi mamʉrigʉn izasari ukumʉya ni ayéy kʉnsámʉse' a'nikwʉyáy, ey awʉn, dikin kwey zwei'nanno.

5.4. LIVING BEINGS AND THEIR USES

Everything that exists on earth, trees, animals, rivers, and humanity have the same relationship and the same traditional law of living; the same applies to for example, lizards, rabbits, ñeque and others.

Everything on earth it depends on our behavior, if we act poorly, the earth and animals would be suffer and decay, and the same apply to us, we are all on earth together.

CHʉKA A'ZʉNA ɈINA A'MʉKANʉYA

Ka'gʉmʉse' inʉ kwey na'ba, ána'nuga, kʉn ɉe awiri unisi zoyeyka, ikʉ eymeygwi nisi zoya name', ka'se' neki a'zabori ʉwari imʉchi awiza neyka, íngwi aná'nuga ka'se' urakʉ ʉngawi zoya neyka Ema zana: Sariwʉwʉ, kuneju awiri asarekʉ.

Ka'gʉmʉse' ayéy re'gawi uzori kwa urakʉ gawi zarisi zamʉ neyka, ka'na'ba inʉ kwey azey azey kwa a'nʉ nánʉya a'mʉkʉnhasi, umʉ́m uzori niwi ikʉ nanʉyáy ka'se', ekari zaku za'na nanʉnno.

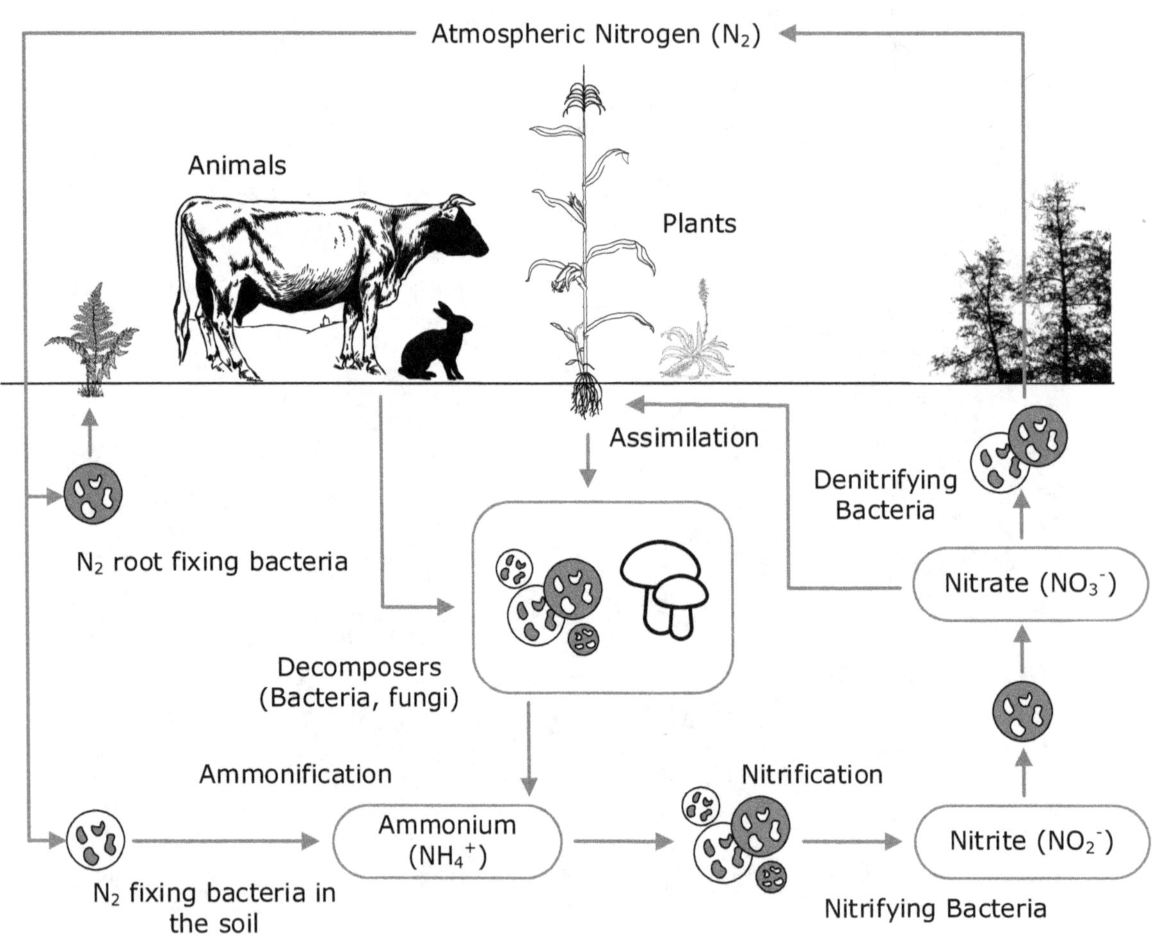

5.5. TRADITIONAL CLASSIFICATION

According to Iku traditions, the soil is classified by its color:

Yellow soil
Red soil
White soil
Black soil

The most productive and fertile is the black soil.

MAMʉRIGʉN ZAKA'CHO'KUMʉYA

Mamʉrígʉndi, ka'ri kawa'ba diwʉ́n diwʉ́n nari rebakwnaki nuga ni:

KA'CHʉMI
KA'ZITI
KA'BUNSI
KA'TWIKAWA

Ka' umʉn zayʉn kʉnáriri umʉ́n pinna a'nigari atwísʉkʉnʉ neyka ni.

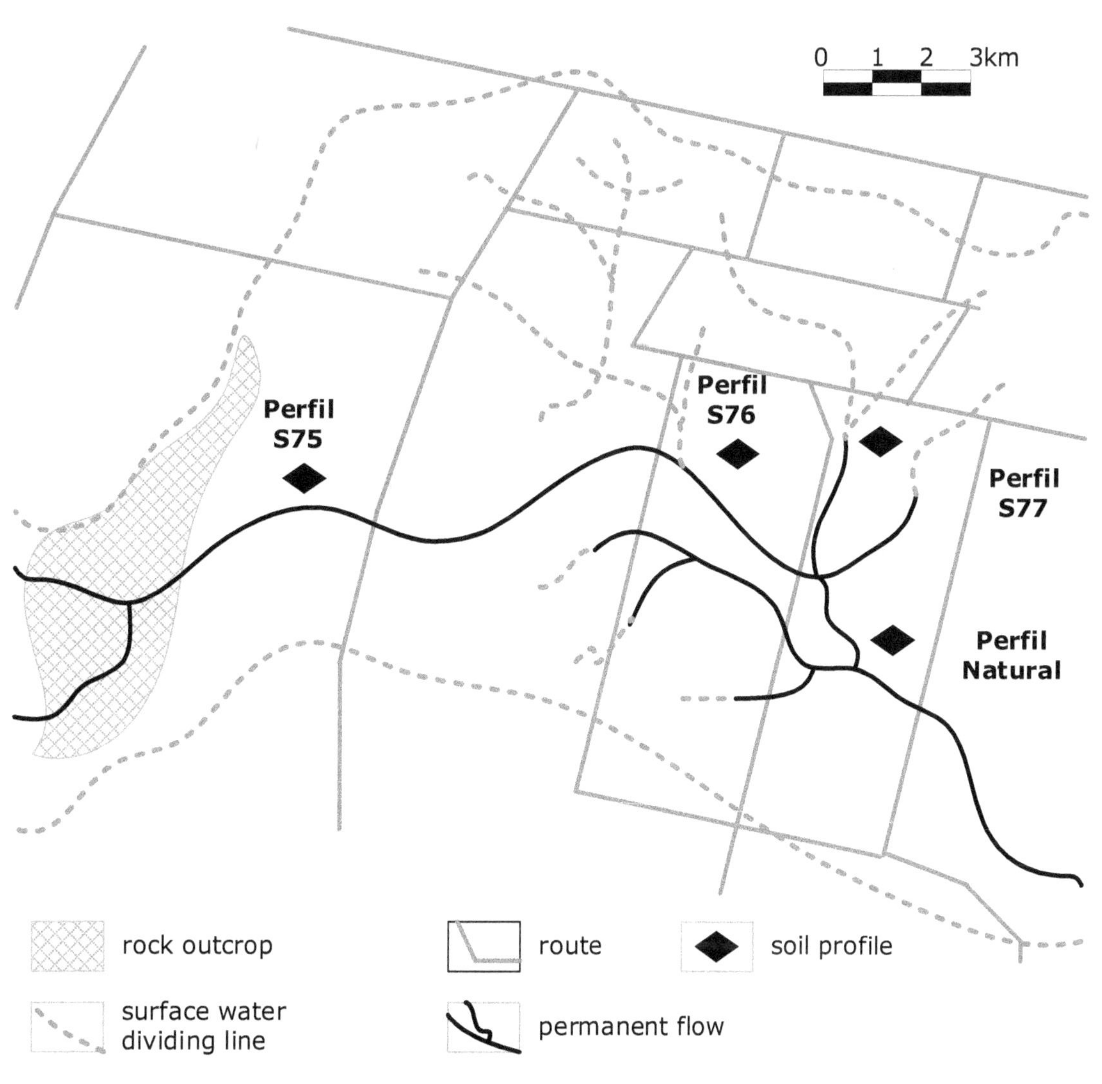

5.6. WESTERN CLASSIFICATION

Western science classifies the soil as:

Muddy	Clay
Sandy	Rocky
Fertile	Dry

Each of these soils has its own characteristics. For example, the clay soil is yellow-reddish and the muddy soil is very wet.

The soil is made up of minerals, water and organic matter.

BʉNACHʉRIGʉN ZAKA'CHO'KUMʉYA

Bunachʉ zʉkunsanʉ siri, ka'ri diwʉ́n diwʉ́n wásʉya ni. Uzu'neyka ka'a'nʉ azu kawa' ka'ɉomʉ neyka, ka'tikʉn neyka ka'ɉuɉʉ neyka, ka' zayʉn kʉnʉnna nenʉ́n zakʉkanuga ni. Ey ʉwe'ri i'ngweti diwiʉ́n diwʉ́n kawa ni, ema zana: ka'ɉuɉʉ neykari chʉmé kawiri ze'ze' kawani. Iwa ka'tikʉn neykari eygumʉn ɉwirí neyka ni.

Ka'neykari ínʉki pinna ɉuna kʉnʉnna ni. Ema zana ɉe', zayʉn, a'nʉ, jieru, oro gunti kʉnʉnna ni.

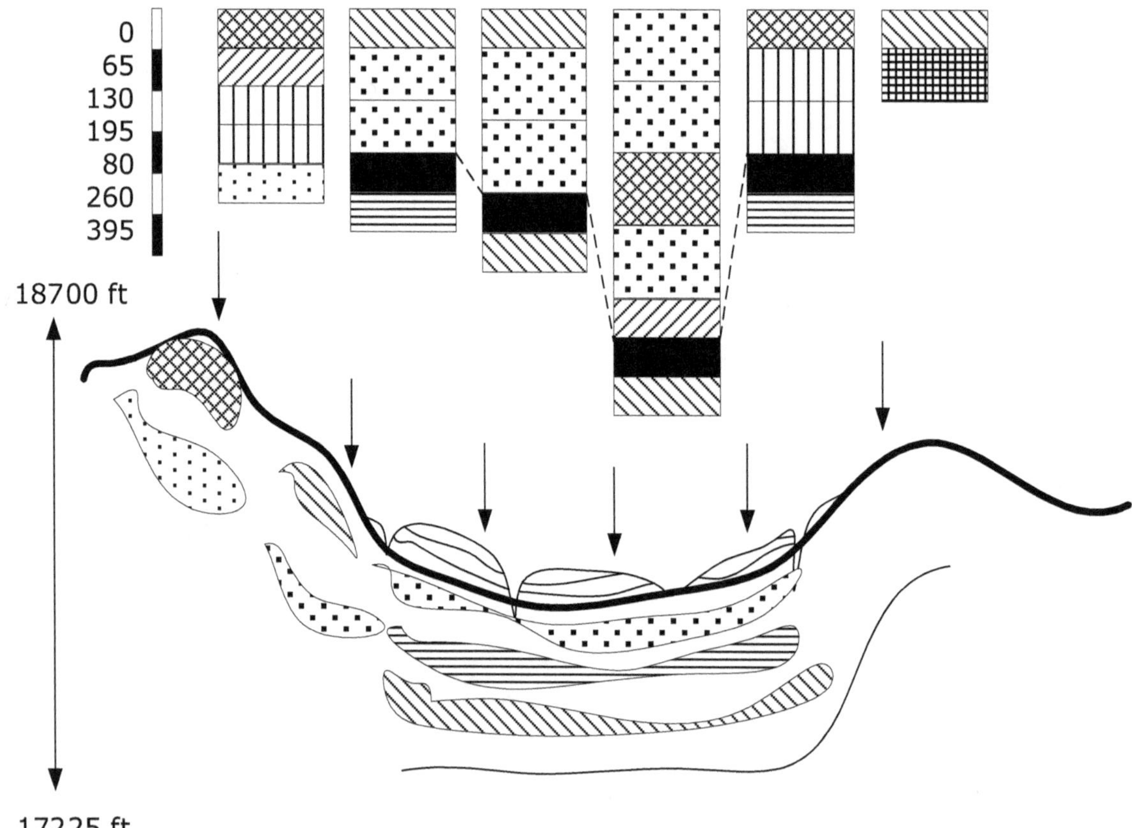

5.7. HANDLING AND CONSERVATION

In general, the Iku perform good soil management; they sow what is necessary for each family and before doing so, they make the proper spiritual tributes or pagamentos.

Defending and protecting the land is something intimate for the Iku, the Earth is something that is related to all beings that exist in nature.

In order to preserve the soil and land, deforestation must be avoided. Only through conservation and through pagamentos we will be able to maintain the equilibrium according to the traditional law.

KA' UZWEYKWA SI AWIRI CHUKWA SI

Ikʉ nʉnkureykari kari du awi chukurome' wa'mʉ nimikumʉ' neyka ni. Nʉkin use mika'mʉkánʉkin zʉn zarisiri ʉyari mamʉrigun ey kinki izasari ukʉmʉya ni.

Ka'gʉmʉ ikwey, azapari ukureykari emi pinna nazey neyka kwʉya, tikumú' nanʉngwasi ey ukumʉya ni.

Ka'gʉmʉ kwey eyki mika'mʉkari zweingwa nʉndi, kʉnkʉnʉ wʉsʉn guasu nari, swʉn gwasu' nari, awi kéywʉri mamʉrigʉn chwi zwein duri na' nʉnno.

5.8. THE SOIL AND ROCKS

According to tradition, there is knowledge to be learned in each stone. Rocks and stones are on earth to achieve a natural balance. They are an important element for the teaching of traditional Science where the diversity of shapes, sizes and colors are recognized. They also differ in their internal properties and energy.

Throughout the Iku indigenous territory, there are many rock formations considered sacred and, therefore, are venerated and respected. Others are simply used for the construction of walls, terraces and roads.

KA' AWIRI A'Nʉ

In'gweti ka'gúmʉse' a'nʉ kwʉyeykari azey azey diwʉ́n diwʉ́n zaka'nuga ni, ʉyari ʉ'umʉkanʉngwa'samʉ kawa ni; ʉya. Ɉinari ka'gʉmʉ tina kwa ʉndérigʉn neyka ni, ínʉki kwey ʉwa chwʉngwari. A'nʉri, kunsamʉ awiri tina chʉzuy nʉneyka ʉnkʉriwiwkwa na' no; kawa' ba (chukirú, ko'kuró, gari kawa, awiri, patiró kawa), eymév anʉwáy azey azey ɉumamʉ kʉnʉna ni.

Niwi ka'gʉmʉse' ri a'nʉ diwʉ́n diwʉ́n zaka'nukʉn nuga kwʉya ni (gwiachʉnʉ a'tínkʉnʉ, kukiamuru a'gomʉ awiri a'chokwa), ʉyari a'zuna name' chow a'chwamu kawa ni. I'ngwi eygwi aykʉnʉri urakuse' amʉkamʉngwa umʉnʉ panʉngwa muraña ʉnkʉnkumʉngwa ingunʉ ʉnbonʉngwa nenʉ́n a'mʉkʉna ni.

5.9. SACRED PLACES

For the Iku, the whole Earth is sacred, but there are special places to which we must observe with special respect. They are sacred sites to avoid all kinds of diseases or problems that can affect the natural balance of things.

Some sacred places are:

KUNCHIAKU KARAKWI
KA'SIMURATU BUNKWANURWA

As we mentioned earlier, the indigenous territory includes everything from the snow peaks at high altitude to the sea and coastal regions, everything within what is considered as the Black Line.

KA' A'ZʉNA KWʉYEYKA

Níwiri ka'ri a'zʉna gunti na'no, ey awe'ki umʉ́n kinki chow a'chwamʉ kawa umʉ́n a'zʉna eygwi kwʉya ni.

ʉya ɟinari pinna ɟuna me'kusi awkwa (wichamʉ bunígʉmʉ) taga'sʉnugazey nari nukʉn nuga na ni.

In'gwí a'zʉneyka ɟina ema ni:

KUNCIDAKU KARAKWI
KAS'SIMURATU BUNKWANARWA

Niwi ka'gʉ́mʉri mʉkuriwakʉ pari chundwa ichona zʉnna ni ʉyari murundwa a'zʉna iminaki nuga'ba undérigʉn neyka na'no.

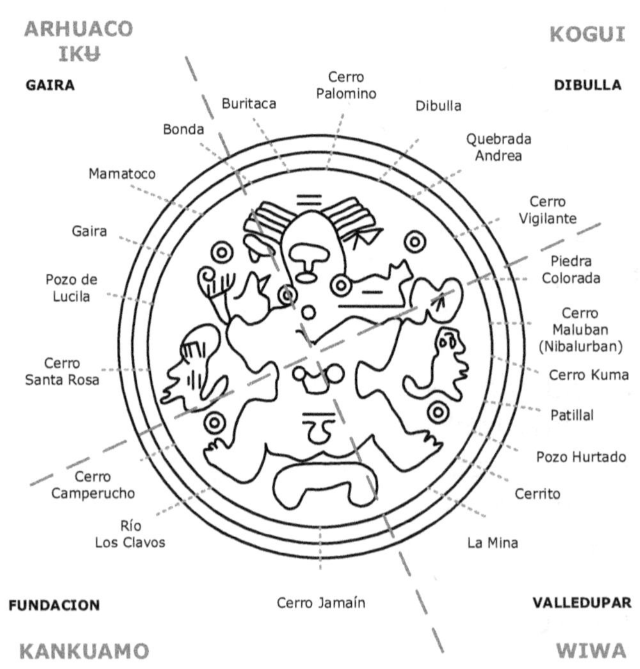

5.10. IMPORTANCE OF THE ROCKS

At the beginning of all things, each object, each being, was assigned with a function to fulfill for itself and for the other species.

For the care of the rocks, the Father of everything commissioned KUNCHANARWA to watch over all the existing stones in the world. SEIA WITUA was specially assigned to protect the flat stones.

On a spiritual level, stones represent the heart of all beings. There are stones that represent humans, and such are used in some ceremonies, such as the A'CHOKWA and the A'GOMU used in weddings. There are also other kinds of stones that represent animals and are used when animals get sick. These stones vary according to the kind of animal, for example: MUNTARI (name of a bush called Jobo).

A'NɄ A'MɄKANɄYEYKA

E' a'bori ukwe'ri azey azey ínʉki kwʉyey kari diwʉ́n diwʉ́n nikamʉ ʉnkuzweingwa nari chukumana na ni; akingwi achungwa nari i'ngwi ayeygwi ni.

Pinna zʉkákʉri, kunchanarwa mamʉ za'kinuga chusana, emi a'nʉ́ neyka ka'gʉ́mʉse' kwʉyeykari chwi angwasi. Ayeygwi nari mamʉ seyawitwo za'kinuga chukumana ʉyari a'nʉ yʉn kama ipá kamazey nari chukumana nʉn. Emi tikʉrigʉn a'nʉri pinna kwʉn nugeyka pinna zʉɉwawika awga ni. Ema se'tagwi nari a'nʉ ikazey nari kwʉya ni.

Ʉya ɉinari diwʉ́n diwʉ́n mamʉrigʉn amʉkʉnani ema zana kichakwa nariri agomʉri jwa ʉnbonʉye amʉkuna ni; emeygwt. a'nʉ, ana'nugazey gwi kwʉyani ʉyarí wichʉkʉpʉnige'i azanʉngwa, ʉyari aná'nuga ɉuna kwʉyáy a'nʉ kwʉya ni ema zana MUNTARI.

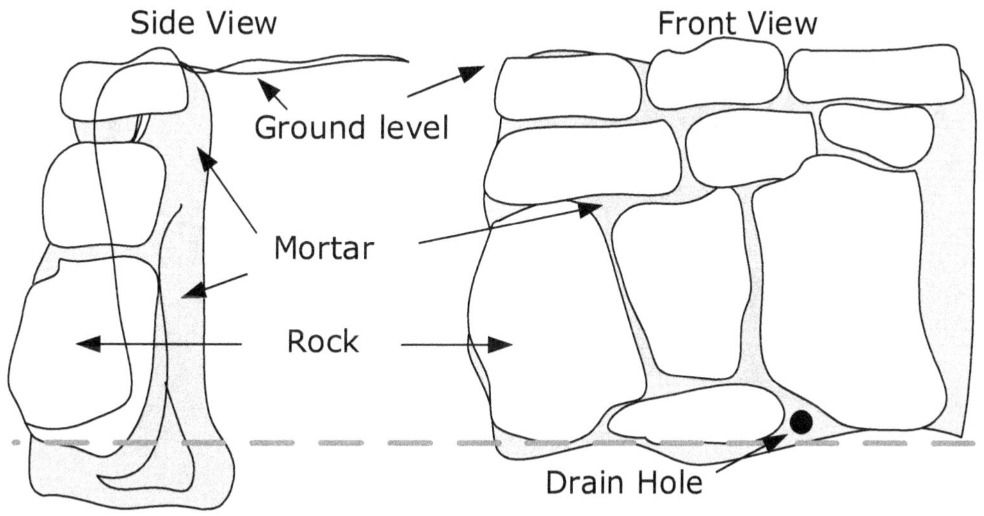

5.11. USE OF THE ROCKS

The vast majority are used for the construction of walls, houses, for the arrangement or construction of roads, while others serve as chairs. There are also special stones able to produce fires such as the ARBONU.

A’MɄKɄNHAKUMɄYA

A'nʉri, muraña ʉngákʉkwa, urakʉ gawkwa, íngunʉ de kʉkunsʉngwari kwa gawʉngwa nari, iásʉkwa, gey achunakumungwa nari arbonu zana, Ʉnkʉzakunʉngwazey nari a'nʉkʉnʉ zano, ayu ʉnpunʉngwazey nari, gunti a'mʉkʉna ni.

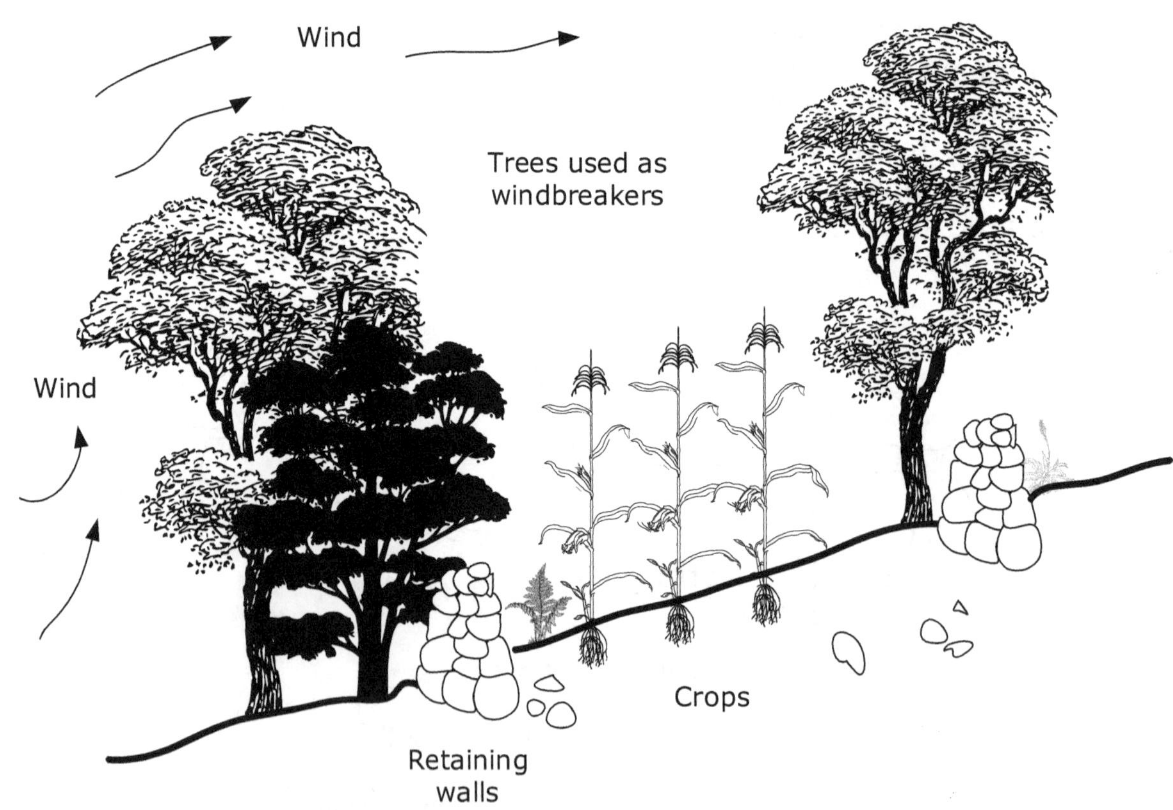

5.12. CLASSIFICATION OF ROCKS

1. Sands
2. Gravel
3. Stones
4. Rocks
5. Peñas

5.13. MEANING OF ROCKS

The small stones in the sea are used in ceremonies paying tribute to the spiritual Fathers. There are stones especially for the KA'DUKWU (stones used by the Mamo and others to sit when in sacred places). Depending on the sacred place from which they are extracted, rocks are used in different kinds of ceremonies. There are cliffs where pagamentos such as GWIÁCHUNU are made, so these rocks represent sites of great spiritual power.

A'Nʉ ɈUNA KWʉYEYKA

1. UZU
2. UZU GRʉNA
3. A'Nʉ ZʉBURU
4. A'Nʉ DOWRU
5. A'TIMOKU

A'ZʉNEYKA

Mʉkuriwase' a'nʉ zʉburu nikwʉ yeykari mamʉ si nikamʉzey nari kwʉya ni zaku kakʉ ɉina ʉnkʉga kawʉngwa nari.

A'nʉ ayeygwi ka' dúkwʉzey nari kwʉya ni.

A'nʉri aguneku párigwi ayeygwi azey azey nikamʉ mamʉnarigʉn kwʉya ni.

A'nʉ gʉrʉtegwi nʉnáy agazásaʉna na ni. ʉyari gwiáchʉnʉ nari umʉ́n jumʉ a'nikwʉya nanʉnno.

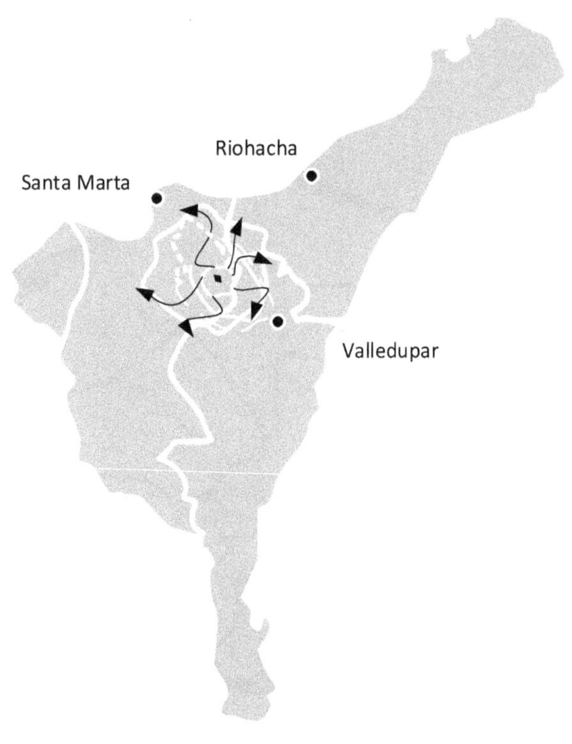

5.14. RESPECT AND CARE

The stones and rocks represent the heart of animals, plants, man and other species. In addition, some are considered the bones of Mother Earth and for this reason we must respect and care for them. Rocks should not be transferred from one place to another without the permission of the Mamos, simply because each rock is fulfilling a mission entrusted to them and based on the site where each one is located.

Misuses of rocks and stones could cause diseases, accidents and even end our lives; that is why when making a construction man must first consult with the Mamo.

CHOW ACHWI AWIRI CHWI AWKWA NEYKA

A'nʉri aná'nuga, kʉn, ikʉn awiri pinna kwʉn nugeyka zʉjwawika na' no zaku seynekʉn zʉwesu name chow achwamʉ awiri chwamʉ kawa na'no a'nʉri yamáy dʉmʉsa awwi'na na'no mamʉ ey mikʉyana nanʉn nʉndi, nikwaʉya'buri amʉkanʉngwari kʉtukʉnʉn chukumanahame name' azi awwi'no na' no.

Kunsumʉ a'nikwʉyáy a'nʉ uzwei' nanʉndi wichamʉ mikunaka, buni'gʉmʉ mikunaka awi kéywʉri manʉnka neki wicha awkwekʉ minichuno na'nuko. Ey ʉwame a'nʉri amʉkanʉngwa sʉn. Gwa neri minsa'gwi mámʉse' izasana awi keywʉ to su' nánuko.

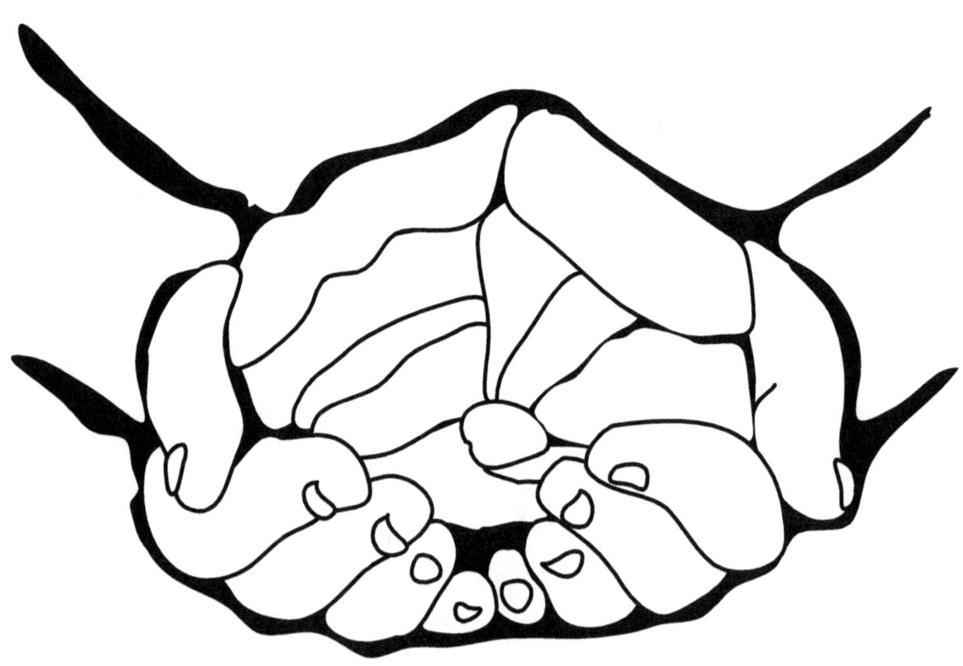

5.15. PEDAGOGICAL ACTIVITIES:

1. What is the name of the stone where the Mamo sits?

2. Draw the various stone classifications in your notebook.

NIKAMʉ

1. Azi za'kinuga no a'nʉ Mamʉ ásʉya'ba.

2. A'nʉ pinna ɨuna paperise' gow awkwa.

AIR AND WATER

6. AIR

6.1. GENERAL GOALS

Highlight and value of the traditional knowledge about Air and its importance for life.

Propose alternatives for air conservation and promote less Air pollution.

6.2. THE AIR (Traditional History)

According to the Iku tradition, everything that exists today was part of the original spirits, and everything was created to fulfill a specific function.

Once air was been created, it was stored in a temple (KANKURWA) in a place called SURIWAKA.

When the the dawn came, the air needed to expand throughout the world, so that all beings (plants, animals and men) could have life.

WAMʉ

EMEY KʉZARI A'KʉMANA NI IZANʉNGWA NEYKA

Kunsamʉ mamʉrigʉn zanʉ ɉwa'si awiri chow a'chwi ema WAMʉ SI wazweingwasi a'kumana ni.

Anʉnkʉsʉkweyna chwi awiri wa'mʉ ikumu ari zweingwa awiri, ga'kʉnamʉ a'chʉnkwasi.

Inʉki kwey ʉwa neykase' ka'mʉkánʉya (kʉn, anánuga, ikʉ) anʉnkʉsʉkweynari anʉme' chosʉkweyna umʉ́n niwikʉɉúnʉya name' niwipáw ɉinase' kwasi zoyana ni, ey ʉwame' eymi pari ikʉ awiri aná'nuga winkwákuma, kʉn bonagwi una ni.

KUNSAMʉ BIRIN ZANʉ

Ikʉzey kunsamʉ ye'ri, yow pinna kwey, chuzarí ʉwaneykari ánugwe nari nʉnna ni.

Yow kwey ʉwa neykari azey azey enʉnay nari a'mʉkana awʉngwasi kwákumey zoyana ní. wámʉri ayeygwi kwákuma awaki nuse'ki. Suriwaka kʉnkurwase' du awaki nu'na ni.

ingʉ ʉnzanika awʉn nuseri bunsi chana una awiri wámʉri zʉnekʉ a'pʉgena awaɉunana emey unuge'ri chʉká a'zʉna ɉinari (kʉn, ana'nuga awiri ikʉ) ayaeygwi ánugwe a'kuma awʉngwasi.

Air is the vehicle of communication and through Air we transmit our thoughts.

Ey ʉwame' ʉya'ba zʉ'n anʉnkʉsʉkwéy nari; kwana ni. Emari bunsichanu'gwi zʉnna ni.

Eymi unsi ʉnchari nare'ri anʉnkʉsi kwéynari pinna aná'nuga, kʉn, ikʉ kwey zweingwá. Siri, pinzʉnay a'pʉgeri zoyana ni. Wámʉri re'no'. Si awkwasi niwika'mʉkʉna, ni.

6.3. IMPORTANCE FOR LIVING BEINGS

The air is one of the essential elements created by the law of origin, and since then life was created.

According to the tradition, it is said that, a dove called JUKARU, flew to the temple where the air was stored and spread it all over the world; that's was how the air was generated according to the Iku traditions. This is the air we breathe and without it, we could not live.

INʉKI KWEY ʉWA NEYKASE' KA'MʉKANʉYA. (kʉn, aná'nuga,ikʉ)

Anʉnkʉsʉkweynari anʉme'chosʉkweyna umʉ́n niwikʉɉúnʉya name' niwi páw ɉinase' kwasi zoyana ni, ey ʉwame' eymi pari ikʉ awiri ana'nuga winkwakuma, kʉn bonagwi una ni.

Niwikunsamʉ birin zanʉ ye'ri in'gwi drúnʉya tana, ɉu'karo za'kinugari suriwaka kʉnkʉrwa nugekʉ anʉnkʉsʉkweyna du ukumana nugekʉ, takʉn, zoyana ni awa ni, umari pinzʉnay ka'tina' kwasʉngwasi. Eméy nari keywʉ anʉnkʉsʉkweyna wamʉ awga neyka, ikwakumana niwikunsamʉse'rí guga ni. Ema wámʉri anʉnkʉkumʉya ni, ey ʉwe'ri ku' nanʉndi kwukwey neki na'nu nanunanno.

6.4. AIR COMPONENTS

Western science discovered that the air is composed of a mixture of gases called: OXYGEN, Nitrogen and Carbon Dioxide.

It is the OXYGEN component we absorve when breathing.

WAMɄSE' ɈUNA KɄNɄNEYKA

Bunachʉ zʉkunsamʉ siri wámʉri diwʉ́n diwʉ́n ɉunase' kwa in'gwi nánʉkin re'gʉwa chwʉzʉnhasa awaki nugari eymey zaka'nuga ni: nitrógeno, OXIGENO y dióxido de carbono.

OXIGENO: Emari wamʉ anʉnkʉkumʉngwa niwi kámʉkʉna ni.

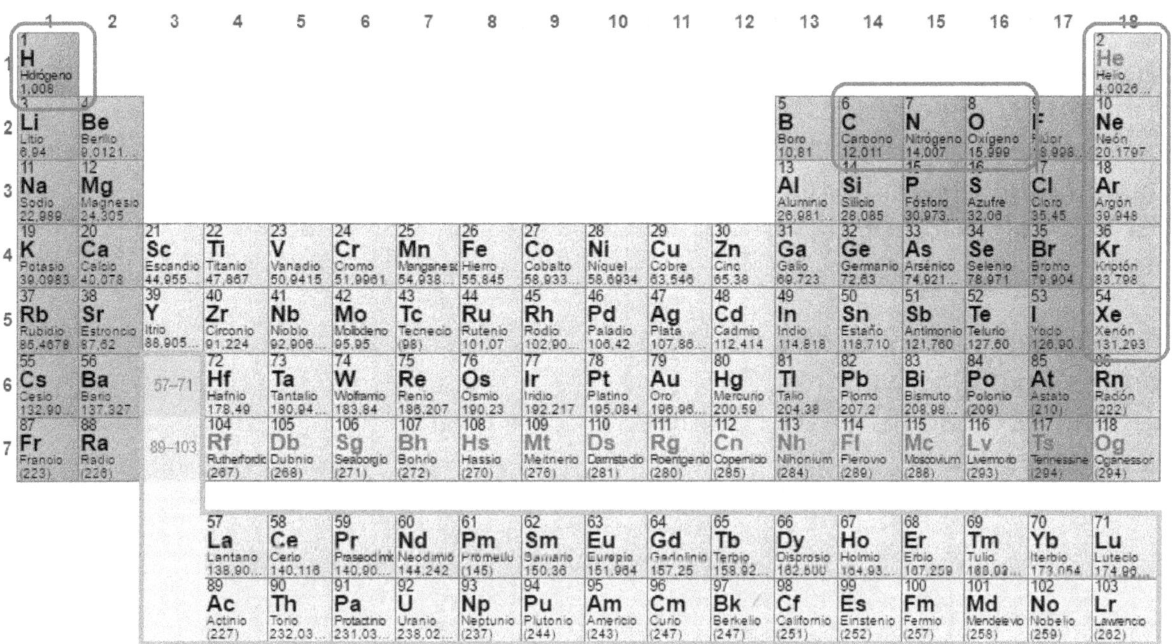

6.5. AIR POLLUTION

Currently, the air is very polluted, especially in cities, this is mainly due to smoke from chimneys, cars and large industries.

All this polluted air cause diseases, destruction of natural resources, deterioration of the ozone layer and much more.

WAMɄ WA'MIKUMɄYEYKA

Iwa se kʉnánʉkwa nanʉndi wámuri bunachʉ zʉ powruse'ri zacha urákʉse' zanʉ, zacha karose'zanʉ awiri inʉki bonʉyekʉ zanʉ, zachari anʉnkʉsʉkweyna wa'mʉ sí zoya ni.

Ema' wamʉ wa'mʉ ikumey zoya nari wichamʉ niwi kunasi pinna kwey ʉwa wa'mʉ sí awiri ema ɉwi ka'se ɉumʉ a'nisi kinkumʉn gwa'su neyka awgeyka ayeygwi.

6.6. PRESERVATION

To preserve air quality, we must be aware that we are all responsible for maintaining and improving the environment around us.

According to the law of origin, we all belong to a single Mother, and it is to her, to whom the Iku must offer tribute, both spiritual and material.

The non-preservation of air brings us consequences and imbalance for life, which then causes a bad relationship between all living beings in our planet.

Air is preserved by taking care of forests, avoiding wildfires, burning vegetation, or by cutting down trees.

WAMʉ CHWAMʉ

Wamʉ chwi zweykwasiri i'ngwikin zaku kwa niwi páw niwi kʉnʉna na' no re'kusa ukure du nanu nanno, zasari ɟwi ekʉzusi zownʉ a'wesi awi uzwein kéywʉri inʉ kinki niwikʉchúkumey awiri a'bori zorie pari niwikunsamʉsin in'gwi nʉkin ikʉ nʉnna niwikʉzaniku'nanno.

Emi anʉ́nkʉsi awkwa neyka chu' nari zweykwa nanʉndi: pinna ɟuna dunanu neyka, wichamʉ, ánugwe mekʉchunhkwa zʉ'n kwákumey zoriza ni, awíkʉchʉ kéywʉri pinna ínʉki kwey ka' ti'na ʉwaneyka ín ayeygwi yówkʉchʉ kʉchonu' nanno.

Anʉnkʉsʉkwéy nari azi awi chwʉkwa nanno me'zanʉndi kʉ́nkʉnʉ chwi, swʉ nari, beysu nari zwein keywʉ e' a'bunnay kawi keywʉri anʉnewesi zwei' nanno.

6.7. PEDAGOGICAL ACTIVITIES:

1. Where does the air originated?

2. Get a balloon, fill it with air from your mouth and then hold it for awhile. Describe what happens.

3. How does air contribute to the health of the human body?

NIKAMʉ

1. Wámʉri bekʉ keywʉ kwakumʉya nanno.

2. Globu ʉnkʉtaka awiri eymi wamʉ ko' re'gow awiri du awa awkwa. Ey unáyuri emey nisin zachʉn a'sa awkwa.

3. Niwigʉ́chʉse' du niwe'zanʉngwari wámʉri azi nisi nwingunámʉsʉnno.

7. WATER

7.1. TRADITIONAL HISTORY

NAWOWA ist he Mother of all waters, she had two children: YUNTANA and JUNKWITI; they began digging in the ground making holes until NAWOWA and KAKU SERANKWA understood that if their children kept digging, those holes would be filled with water and people would not have where to live. Then NAWOWA and SERANKWA formed hills and mountrains where there was still flat land available.

While streams are called younger children of NAWOWA, large rivers are considered older children.

In sacred places, water should not be collected with pots such as metal containers, pans and jars, because Water will get scared and go back to the Mother. In these cases, pumpkin shells and totumas are used for collection.

JE'

KUNSAMɄ BIRIN ZANɄ

Ɉe' zákuri NAWOWA za'kinuga ni. Ʉyari mowga gʉmʉsinʉ kʉnʉna: YɄNTANA awi ɈEKWITI; I'mʉnʉ kéywʉri agʉmʉsinʉ ɉinari ka' winkwisʉn pana keywʉ winuna, ey uye'ri NAWOWA Serankwasin wina'zareri ka' kwisi zwein pʉnna kínkiri.

Ɉe' ka'zanisiri yow íkʉri kukwey neki winikizanu awkinanno keywʉ wina'zʉnna. Ey uye'ri Serankwa Nawowasindi gwirʉkʉnʉ gawʉn pana winowna, ey uye' nʉnkʉri ka'ri yow sʉwanʉ zʉ'n zʉnna.

Ɉecho' awgeykari Nawowa zʉ gʉmʉsinu awʉ' a'zʉna nʉnna ni iwa
ɉeswi zari zoyaki nugari gʉmʉsinʉ eygumʉn a'zʉna nʉnna ni.

Beki azasari zoya'ba, u'mʉnʉ neki pʉnsi zʉna'bari Ɉeri beki pótisin, pastasin prátusin neki a'gíkʉkwey neyka nanu neyka ni, emey awʉndi gakʉmeyri azaku sikʉ ʉ'bunnekʉ ʉnzoya ni. Emey ʉwame' sosin, chókwʉsin zʉn a'gikʉn du nariza ni.

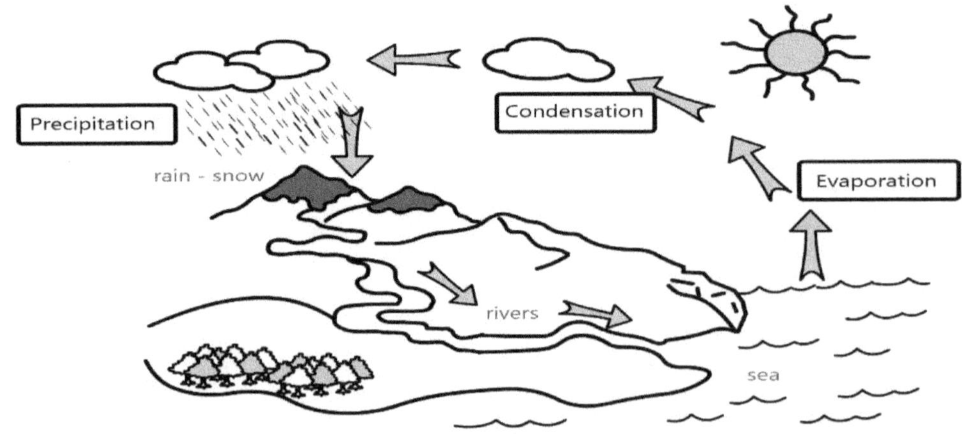

7.2. WATER: TRADITIONAL MEANING

There are many similar things that surround us and, at first glance, they seem the same, but analyzing them in more detail we see that each one fulfills a different function. So you can think about rivers, the sea, lagoons, springs, streams and all those places where water passes by, places where is born, or where is hold. Although all of them contain water, they have a different cultural meaning, even thouh they keep a connection to each other.

Let's look at some definitions to understand these concepts a little bit better:

7.2.1. RIVERS

Within the Iku culture, rivers are a long spiritual path that has several gates. In that regards, all souls have to travel a path similar to rivers when their body dies. If a person dies and has been carrying the tradition well, his soul will not have any delay in their journey and when they reach the last door, they will be able to join Father KAKU SERANKWA.

On the other hand, if a person dies and was not complying with the traditional law, his/her soul will take a long time to reach the end of the journey. Mainly because he/she will have to pay tributes in each gate, and so, by the time he arrives at the last

NIWIKUNSAMɄ SI ZAKA'NUGA ɈINA

Ɉeswí, Mʉkuriwa, Ɉiwʉ, Ɉecho' Inʉki neki ɉina zʉ'n du kʉnana'nu nari zun chwʉkwa nanʉn kínkiri diney kawáy gunti ʉwanu' nánʉko, ey ʉwe'ki tikʉrigʉnkin chukwa nanʉndi azey azey diwʉ́n diwʉ́n a' mʉkanʉkweyna winʉkʉna ni. Eymase' ta warʉnukwey niku'nanno; mʉkuriwa, ɉeswi, ɉecho, ɉiwʉ, emari sigʉ́n kʉzagichʉn kwa tin ne nikʉnki tikʉrigʉn kinki azey azey zaka'nuga nanʉnki agwi gunti nanay niga ni.

Umʉn niwikuwa'nʉngwásiri azey azey neyka zaka'chó kumʉya ni.

JESWI

Emi niwikunsamʉ siri ɉe' kínkiri íngunʉ nani awga ni, íngunʉ yamʉn yamʉn gumʉ a' nisi ikʉ neki ʉnwicha awʉndi eymitá ánugwe ʉnzoya awga ni.

In'gwi ikʉ keywʉ wicha awiza nanʉndi ikʉrigʉndi ɉe'ri íngunʉ na ni awga nanʉndi eymiri ánugwe kachwi wazoya ná ni, du arunhʉya nannʉndi ingunʉndi katigu kari ukumu gwawa nari akowna o'kʉ'ɉu chanʉkwekʉ kinkuma ʉ'wa ni; eymiri azey azey ʉnkwʉngwarigʉn ʉndebónʉya ni ey unige'ri niwi páw kakʉ serankwa sikʉ kinkumʉya ni du arunhanari. Iwa ánugwe du a'niku nari zoyana nanʉndi ingwi nari zwei' nari yamʉn yamʉn akʉyʉ kʉnugay

gate he is purified and can join KAKU SERANKWA in the CHUNDWA (place where the spirit arrives and is reaches the last snowy peak).

zasari ɉina anuni'na anʉnchunʉn keykumey zoya ni emari akowna kinkumayeri kunuku' nari kinkumeyri kakʉ serankwasin chundwakʉ ʉnzweingwasi.

1. Magdalena River
2. Orinoco River
3. Black River
4. Amazon River
5. Madeira River
6. Tapajós River
7. Xingú River
8. Tocantins River
9. San Francisco River
10. Paraguay River
11. Paraná River

7.2.2. THE SEA/OCEANS

At the beginning everything that is on Earth today, was occupied by the sea, even the high altitudes and the snow peaks (vary sacred for the Iku), but throughout time, oceans retreated to where they are today.

All things originated from the sea/ocean, for this reason, she is considered the Mother of everything that exists in the universe.

At the sea, pagamentos (offerings or tirbutes) are made to all things as well as to LWAWIKU, ARWAWIKU, ATISEYNINTE, and SEYWKWIN, names of spiritual forces that maintain oceans, and that also represent the cardinal points north, south, east and west.

Many materials are brought from sea to land, and used both in traditional works/tasks, and also in spiritual activities.

Among the different materials that are brought from sea to land, we can mention some such as GUN, JO'SA and JO'TINWU (names of sea snail types) which are used as tribute elements in pagamentos.

Currently, access to the ocens near Sierra Nevada de Santa Marta is distributed as follows: from Palomino to Riohacha, is

MʉʼKURIWA

Kʉtʉkʉnʉndi iwa ka'chuzʉna kínkiri mʉkuriwa zʉn pinzʉnáy chuzʉna ni. Ey unayu ɉwʉn ɉwʉn uyuri zoyanari iwa ʉnnʉna'ba kinki chukumana. Mʉkuriwase' pari pinna ɉuna kwákuma zoya nani ey ʉwame' pinna emey ka'gʉmʉ ɉina kwey ʉwa neykari pinna zakʉ ʉnkʉwʉnkura ni.

Mamʉrigʉn gwákʉkwa nanʉndi mʉkuriwiákʉri arwawiku. IWAWIKʉ, ATI SEYNEKʉN, SEYUKWIN, ATI SEYNINTE zana nari ɉwi ekʉzusi wazoya ni. Eymi pariri eymekʉ zanu a'buru kwa na' nandi eykʉ zasanʉkwéy zanʉndi uyéy awi wazoya ni, emari ɉwi a'chónʉya se kʉnari.

A 'buru mamʉse' kʉɉúnʉya mʉkuriwakʉ pari wanʉgeykari ema
ni: gun, ɉo'sa, ɉo'tinwʉ awiri eyki na ni.

Mʉkuriwari niwi kunsamʉ siri ey méy kawi niwi kʉchukúmey zoyana ni parominu pari Riwacha kindi kʉgʉwa awiri wiwa zey nari, iwa parominu pariri gaira kindi wintukwa zey ema ney kari.

Máykʉnʉ ɉuna ikʉ nʉnkureykari inʉki niwi kʉɉúnʉya awiri a'mʉkanʉngwasi wa zweingwa; zaku ɉinari emey kawi Niwi kʉchukumana ni ey ʉwame' zaku nikwʉyékʉri poso colorado za'kinuga ni makuriwazey nari azasanʉyekʉ.

used by the KOGI and WIWAs, and from the Palomino river until Gaira river, is used by the Arhuaco or IKU. Thus, the three ethnic groups can make use of the sea and all its content. The Mother of the Sea is located on the site that today is known as COLORADO WELLS near the city of Santa Marta.

7.2.3. LAGOONS

Although several lagoons con be found in the Sierra Nevada de Santa Marta, each one of them has a different meaning to the Iku people, and all of them are important within the Iku tradition.

The NAWOWA lagoon is considered the Mother of water. She is constantly moving to send water to all parts of the world, just as the heart moves in our body and send the blood to our entire organism.

Of the many lagoons in the Sierra Nevada, we could highlight the following: ATI KONKERA, ATI GUNDIWA, and ATI MUNDIWA. Some special stones from these lagoons are used in weddings. Such stones are known as ACHO'KWA.

There is a permanent spiritual communication between the Sea and the Lagoons. All the tribute elements moved from the Sea to the Lagoons and viceverse, are known as A'BURU.

ɈIWʉ

Du se kʉnanʉndi chundwákʉri diwʉ́n diwʉ́n zaku ikwʉya nari keywʉri azey azey ɉwi ékʉzusi zweykwey neyka ne'ki yow niwizeyri a'zʉna gunti na ni.

Ɉiwʉ Nawowa za' kinugari zʉnʉ kin dʉmʉnʉn nusiri pinsʉnáy emi ka' ɉina ɉe' kwʉngwa re'gawi zoya ni inʉ ne gwákʉkwa nanʉndi niwiɉwawikari pinzʉnáy niwigʉ́chʉse' ɉwa gá'suya nanʉndi eyma zana gwi nari a'mʉkʉna ey awga ni.

Umʉnʉkʉnʉ síkʉri ɉiwʉ zari zoyaki nugari ingʉ zʉguró winneyka ni. In'gwiri Ati mʉ́ndiwa, awga na'no. Ey ʉweri eymeka gun a'nʉ mamʉse' kʉjunʉya kwʉn nuga ni. Eyma a'nʉri, a'chokwa awga, ɉwa ʉnbonʉye' kʉjunʉya ni. Mʉkuriwa nariri ɉiwu sindi dikin windeno'si zoya ni. A'buru mʉkuriwakʉ zánʉri ɉiwʉ Sikʉ ʉnwazoya ni, iwa ɉiwʉ sikʉ zanʉ mʉkuriwakʉ.

7.2.4. SPRINGS

These are the places where we can see that water simply flowing to the surface of Earth. This can occur between rocks and stones, or simply from the subsoil in fertile areas.

Springs have special meanings based on their location and cardinal orientation, these are some of them:

For those Springs oriented to the north, is considered that their waters are faithful, pure, in a good traditional sense, therefore, their waters are used for ceremonial events such as the baptism of newborns and other good luck celebrations.

The waters from eastern-facing Springs are used for blessings and ceremonial events related to good future. These springs are usually centralized and their waters are distributed to other areas of the territory. Tributes are made to the four cardinal points using these waters.

The waters of the southern-facing Springs are used to clean the entire body and other things.

On the other hand, the western spring waters are used for mortuary baths and other necessities. Also, because they are considered weak waters, compared with the other Springs, the waters from all the other cardinal points have to help the

ɈECHO'ɈINA

Ema ɉecho' kwey Kari ɉe pies zoyeyka ey awgani ʉyari azey azey gwi nari izasánʉkwey neyka ey agwaku' nanno, diwʉ́n diwʉ́n ká' tina chwʉzʉna'ba.

Ema jʉna neykari bemáy pari nakʉndi ʉya Kiay sekʉnʉna ni ema zana:

Arusi kiay yunʉndi duna nani. Ey ʉwame' umʉ́n kinki amʉse' a'mʉkanʉngwasi uzoya na ni. Ema zana gʉmʉsinʉ ɉwa kʉkumʉye' awiri pinna ɉuna a'buru ukumʉye, eyma ɉe mika'mʉkánʉkwa ni.

Iwa ɉwi a'chunárigʉn pari yunʉyeykari du zari zweykwa nariazásʉna na ni. Emari umʉ́n du nari pinzʉnáy zanʉ nanʉkin nari yuri zoya ni. Iwa ɉwi anʉkʉmʉchʉyárigʉn zánʉri ga'ʉnbori zoye' awiri du ʉnkʉkumey zoye' kʉjunuya nani.

Iwa yuri kwa wari'gʉn gwákʉkwa sírigʉn pari ipesʉyari Eysa anukumey zoye' kʉɉúnʉya nani. Ey uweri emari umʉ́n ɉumʉ a'niku nari arusi zanʉ, ɉwi a'chunáy zánʉri ɉwi kʉmʉchʉyáy zanʉse'ri igunámʉsi zoya ni; ey unige'ri dikin ʉnkʉngunámʉsi rizweingwasi.

western springs to maintain the traditional balance with the universe.

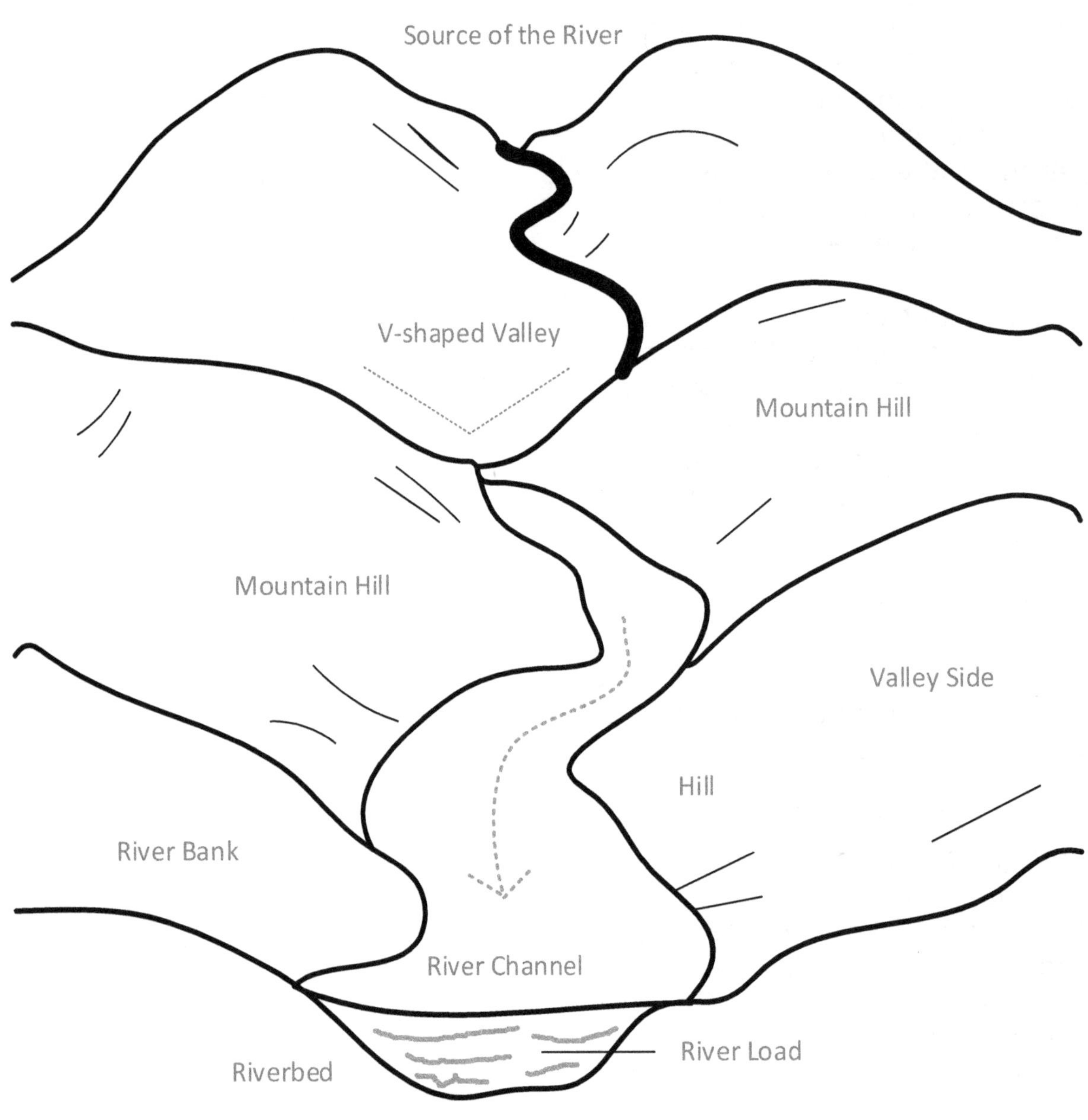

7.2.5. STREAMS

Just as in our body there are a number of thick and thin veins, and even some thinner veins, all carrying blood to the smallest parts of our body, so there are streams on the ground. They are a network of conduits through which water flows to all regions of the territory.

Usually, streams have their origin at the footing of a tree, near a natural fault in a mountain, under a stone, or on the edge of a ridge; and although initially only a minimum amount of water sprouts, its flow increases as it travels thorugh land, mainly thanks to other streams and water sources that add to it. At the end of their tour, they reach a river or the sea.

ɈE' ZɄGɄMɄ

Emi niwigʉ́chuse' se ʉnkʉnánʉkwa nanʉndi ɉwasía niwi kʉnari chine hi neyka zuzukin neyka awiri umʉ́n zu' neyka niwikʉnari zoyeyka, eymay azey azey ɉwa kʉnari zoyéki.

Anʉnni'kumey zoriri a'kowna gʉchʉ niwikʉnʉnékʉkin kinkumey zoya na ni. Ey ʉwame' eymase' tá gwi nari ɉe zʉgʉmʉ ɉinari yamʉn gamʉngwi ɉe kʉnari zoriri ʉnni'kumey zoye'rí ɉe' swi sikʉ kʉchari, ey mi pariri umʉ́n ɉe'zari zoyaki nugekʉ mʉkuriwa sikʉ kʉchánʉya ni.

7.3. COMMON USE OF WATER

Preparing food, washing our clothes, bathing, providing drinking water to animals and humans, are the most common uses water on a daily basis. Furthermore, water is used to keep crops healthy, wash kitchen utensils, fruits, wash coffee and other activities.

Although these are daily activities, there should always be a spiritual permit and only obtain the water from an auhorized location or source.

SIGIN JE' A'MʉKʉNA

Ema ɟe' neykari sigin ey uwin me'zánʉkwa ne nʉnʉnki ʉya gun anʉme'chá' sʉya guneri diwʉ́n diwʉ́n ʉnniwi ka'mʉkanʉngwa na'no. Ema ɟuna a' ey awkwa'ba, awmey awkwa'ba ana'nugase' a'kawi awkwa, ʉnkʉzarosi, a'wkwa'ba, nari guntí, eygwi umʉ́n pinna ɟunazey ɟe' kínkiri niwika'mʉkari zoya nánno ey ʉweki Sigin niwikamʉkánʉya ni, ne awanʉnki, áykʉnʉ zaku ikwey zuya gun nanʉndi ʉya izasari ʉnka'zasisamʉ mi gʉnkwʉn du na' nanno.

7.4. CEREMONIAL USE

Water is an element of great importance for the performance of ceremonial tasks.

Based on the task at hand and the intended use, the Mamo will establish from which source it can be collected.

Water is so used in ceremonial activities that, to describe all possible uses this unit, it would be too extensive, however, we can explain some of the most important ones.

7.4.1. CEREMONIAL USE OF WATER WHEN A CHILD IS BORN

When a child is born, the Mamo establishes where you can go to get the water. This water must be collected in a pumpkin shell or totuma. These waters are usually brought from springs in the northern part of the Sierra Nevada, as these waters are cisidered of great spiritual power.

The water used cannot be disposed anywhere. Once used, it is collected again, and then buried by the Mamo.

After the initial bath and blessing by the Mamo, the child can bath in any other source of natural water.

MAMʉSI ɈE A'MʉKʉNA

Ɉe' kínkiri binzari nenʉ́n ka'mʉkánʉya na'nanno mamʉ sí a'buru ukumʉye' nʉnkʉri kʉjunʉyákʉchʉgwi gun nanʉndi.

Ema ɉe' agusi awízʉna mámʉse, eymekʉpari gukʉkwéy nariza ni gwaku'nunno mámʉse' achunaki nu'nige. Ɉe' kínkiri mamʉ riwʉn kínkiri pinna ɉunazey a'mʉkʉna' ni; ey ʉweri yow a'sʉkwa umʉngwi gari nisiza name', umʉn ɉwa'kumʉkwéy neyka zʉn emi zaka'chósukwa ni.

GʉMʉSINʉ KWAKUMʉYE' AMʉKANʉYA

Gʉmʉsinʉ kwákumuye zoye'ri ɉwa anʉkʉkumey zweingwásiri mámuse' guge'ri: "kúrigʉn kiay zanʉ ɉecho' yʉ́nuya gukʉkwa awgani", e mi pariri ʉyari umʉ́n kumʉ a'nisi ɉumamʉ kʉnʉna awga ni, yow ema ɉe' wanasi awizeykari pótise unaku' nari sose' chókwʉse' unákʉkwa awgani.

Ema ɉe gʉmʉsinʉ ʉnkwákumey zoya neykari yanké'kʉchʉ wite awkwey na'nu neyka ni ʉyari mámʉse', aseynáriri ka,' anisa zʉn ʉwa ni.

Ey unayu nʉngwari, gʉmʉsínʉri bema ɉese' neki anukwásʉkwey nanu nanno.

7.4.2. CEREMONIAL USE OF WATER WHEN A WOMAN GIVES BIRTH TO A BABY

Just after a woman gives birth, she cannot bath in any natural water source. The water for that first bath after delivery, is brought from a spring indicated by the Mamo. That water is brought in squash shell or totuma. After the woman takes this bath, that water is collected to be buried along with the baby's placenta and the water used to bath the newborn.

Both the child's and the mother's baths are necessary to present them before the ancestral Fathers.

GWATI GɄMɄSINɄ ɄNKɄTOSɄYE' A'MɄKɄNA

In'gwi gwati ʉnkʉzato ʉwe'ri yʉnkekʉchʉ ɉe'se' owma neki awkwey na'un neyka ni. Owmʉngwa kínkiri, mámʉse' ɉecho' ipesʉyekʉ pari unákʉkwa ɉe kínkiri sose', kwa chókwʉse' zʉ'n unákʉkwey niga ni.

Gwátiri anʉnkʉzato anʉwe'ri ɉe anowmanari, ɉe gʉmʉsʉ anowmanasin nariri akʉnkáwʉsin yow ka' anasi mamʉse'ri ʉwa ni.

Yow ɉe ana'mʉkanʉngwa' kumanari zaku sikʉ anizazánʉkwa mamʉse'ri kʉnisi zoya ni, ey ʉweri gʉmʉsinʉ ʉnkwakumana nariri azaku anukwákumey zoyeykari zayʉn nisi zoya ni.

7.4.3. CEREMONIAL USE OF WATER WHEN A YOUNG GIRL STARTS HER DEVELOPMENT AS A WOMAN

When a young woman or adolescent begins to develop as a woman, she must inform her mother so she will then notify the Mamo. The Mamo will be responsible for giving her first SEYMUKE bath.

After doing the ceremonial work, the Mamo will tell the young lady where she can bath. There, the young woman will draw the water from the pumpkin shell or totuma, usually taken from a stream or river, and sit in a KUNKAWU, assigned by the Mamo. With the help of the mother or another woman, she will start pouring water from the head to her feet. Once this bath is finished, the young woman will be recognized as a woman and will no longer be a girl before the eyes of the community and the traditional law.

After the bath of SEYMUKE, she can bath in any river or stream that she deems convenient. The water used in the SEYMUKE is called MITUKWA.

Such water must not be thrown back to the ground, but deposited in an appropriate vessel and then be taken by the Mamo to a place he has chosen for final dispossal.

GAYSINʉ ACHʉNA NISI ZOYE A'MʉKʉNA

Gáysinʉ achʉna nisi zoye'ri azaku keywʉ kʉya awnanno; ey unige'ri mamʉse'ri anukwasi séymʉke re'gawʉngwasi. Yow nikamʉ anekʉchuna ukumʉye'ri, mamʉse'ri eymekʉ owmʉn zweykwey neyka ni, eymékʉri so'sin kwa chókwʉsin zʉn agikʉkwéy neyka ni, éymiri azákuse' igunamʉsiri sakʉn minsʉ
ingiti ʉndosi keywʉ ówmʉya ni. Ey awiri ɉe anowmanari yʉnke kʉchʉ dósʉkwey neki na' na ni, beki yow a'do unájuri mámʉse ' eymekʉ uzweykwey kawin a'zʉneri ayéy awi uzoya ni.

Yow nikamʉ anʉkʉchona anʉwé nʉngwari, mamʉse'ri be neki awmʉkwéy ni gwa' ʉweri gaysʉnʉse' anowma a'ɉunʉya'ba, anowmʉkwéy neyka ni.

Gáysʉnʉ achʉna ne'ri ɉe anowmanari: MITUKWA AWGA NI.

7.4.4. CEREMONIAL USE OF WATER IN MORTUARY CASES

When someone dies, their children, wife or husband, and all other mourners, have the traditional obligation to purify their bodies and souls so as not to have problems in the future. For such spiritual cleaning act, a purification bath is required.

Such purification bath is managed by a Mamo. This kind of bath is also known as EYSA and depending on the way the person died, so will the work of cleaning and spiritual purification. For example, when the person dies naturally, family members can bath in any well prepared by the Mamo. However, if the person dies violently, the EYSA must be performmed in the BUTISINU wells.

EYSA UKUMʉYE A'MʉKANʉYA

Bema neki wichi zoye'ri asinamʉ ɉinari. Yow du ʉnkʉkusʉkwa niga ni; emari tʉkin pariri umʉn du wina'zari.

Mamʉ ema eysa chwi zweingwa neykari kʉɉunʉyase' ʉnkaguna neyka ni.

Yow eyma nikamʉ kunsámʉse' kwʉyari eysa awga ni ʉyari azi nisi wichanandi ʉya sekʉnari gun mámʉse'ri chwʉya ni.

Inʉ negwákʉkwa nenanʉndi bema neki wichamʉsínkʉchʉ wicha owna nanʉndi be neki owmʉkweykʉchʉ kʉnʉnani, ey ʉwe'ki gʉmeynari wichʉye' nʉngwari ɉese' butisinʉ niga'ba owmʉkwa kʉniga ni. Ey ʉwe'ki emari yow mamʉse' eyméy guga ni.

Ɉe' waséykʉmey zoya'bari in'gwiri umʉnkʉchʉ chow a' chwi zweykwey neykagwi kwey zoya ni. In'gwi zakachosʉkwa nandi: ɈWI KʉNOWMA ema kínkiri mamʉ sírigʉndi péykʉchʉ a'zʉna neyka ni, yamʉn yamʉn ɉe a'kwey zoyaki nugay re'masi win zoya ni.

Yow ema neykari chow a'chwi gunti zoríkure du kaw'nanno, owmákʉchʉ neki aw'nari, nʉkin mámʉse' gwa' únige'.

7.4.5. OTHER IMPORTANT USES OF WATER

There are other important sites, such as JWIKUNOWMA wells, which are of great significance for the spiritual communication between wells in different places.

These wells deserve respect and, in addition, people should not bath in them without prior authorization from the Mamo.

IN'GEYGWI NA'BA' ɈE A'ZʉNA NÍ AWÁNʉKWA.

In'geygwi nanke ɉe awʉtari a'zʉna ní awánʉkwa neykari, in'geygwi ɉe a'kwey kwaré zari a'kwey zoyari ɈWIKʉNOWMA za'kinuga ni. Ema neykari zʉnekʉ ɉwikʉnowma a'kwey zoyari winde'rigʉnsi winde'rinugga ni awga ni.

Ema ɉe kwaré zʉneykari chow a'chwamʉ kawa ni awgani. Mámʉse' agʉnku nari owmákʉchʉ awnánʉkwa awga ni.

7.5. WATER CYCLE

For all cultures, both native and western, this concept of the Water Cycle is very important. Well, without enough water sources for human or animal consumption, we would all die. The same happens if water sources are contaminated or destroyed.

When portions of water from rivers and oceans evaporate, it rises to the atmosphere in the form of gas. There, in the atmosphere, it accumulates in the clouds and returns again to its liquid state. Then, it drops from the clouds and falls into the ground in the form of rain or snow. It will fall back into rivers and oceans to repeat the evaporation stage again; which would start once again the Water Cycle.

ꞫE DIWɄN DIWɄN NIGA

Beki Ɜe'swi awiri kwa mʉkuri'wa neki Ɜwise' ɟumʉ a'nisi chwʉyeri wiwi aza'ninaɟuri wamʉ nari kingwi warin atmosferas ayekʉ zoya ni, ey mekʉ pari eygwi ɟe'.

Ʉnnigeri ɟewʉ ʉnnari ʉnwá'nʉya ni, ey awiri eymi paririri, eygwi ayeygwi eygwi ayeygwi zʉ́n sigin niga ni.

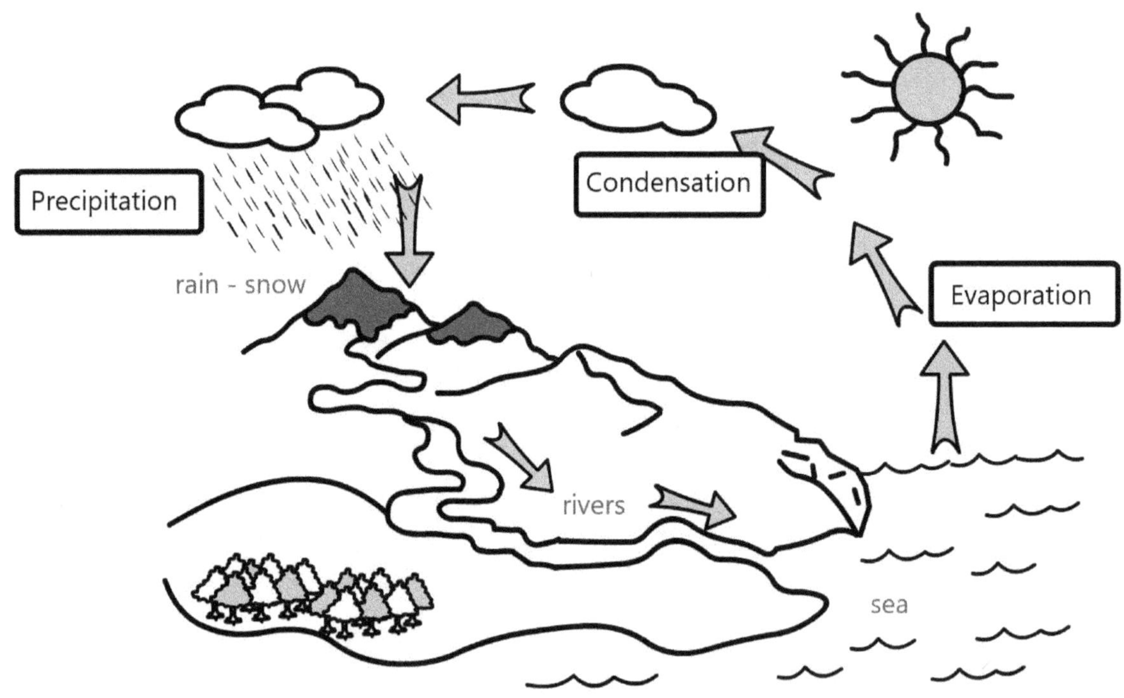

7.6. WATER CONTAMINATION

There are many ways to contaminate water. In some cases, pollution is slow and in others fast. Let's look at some cases:

In the past, indigenous people did not use chemical products to wash clothes or for personal or animal bathing. After Western cultures brought the soap, it was used by the natives as well as disinfectants, shampoo and many other products used for cleaning clothes and personal hygiene.

Unfortunately, these products can cause contamination in many aspects.

However, there are more serious cases of water pollution in cities, for example. In cities, some people throw garbage and chemical waste into the drainage systems or the environment, thus causing the death of fish, birds and plants.

With the increase in water pollution there will be more environmental problems, diseases, and even death and desolation.

ꞴE' WA'MIKUMEY

Ꞵe' wa'mʉ isi awkwa kínkiri, diwʉ́n diwʉ́n nisi wa'mísʉkwa kwʉya ni. Ey ʉwe'ri niwi ikʉ nʉnkureykari birindi ínʉki bʉnáchʉse' owmey neki aw' nʉnna ni.

Eymi pariri tʉkindi bunachʉ ʉnkinkumeyri mʉkʉ agáchukwʉya ʉnniwikunakʉn pana, beki sakʉn re'bechʉkweyna ayeygwi anunakʉn pana gwi anawi zorie'ri, ikʉ se'ri, uya du ʉnmikʉnikʉn pana gwi anawi ʉnzorie' kinki, ɉe'ri manʉnka kingwi wa'mʉanisi ɉe' kínkiri wa'mʉ anisi zʉn ʉnzoyáy niku nanno.

Ey ʉwe'ki eygwi umʉ́n du na'neyka, ɉe' wa'misʉkwa ey kwʉya ni. Beki bunachʉ keynari ínʉki diwʉ́n neyka diwʉ́n neyka bunna yʉnke ɉese' kʉwitesi zoye' kínkiri pinna ɉese' kwey ʉwa kínkiri wichi zʉ'n gwʉn zweindi, awiri eyma imʉ na'nari dirúnʉya, wakʉ ɉina awiri kʉn ɉʉna kwey ʉwa neyka a kingwi zoya ni.

Niwi ne eygwi yow ɉe wa'mʉ isi zwein pana awkwa nanʉndi eygumʉn wichamʉ kwakumeyri, anawichi azwein pariza ni.

7.7. WATER CONSERVATION

Water needs a lot of care so that it does not disappear from the natural environment.

Indigenous people in general have been very careful in protecting natural resources, especially water.

Within the Iku culture, the best way to protect the water is to make the pagamentos (spiritual offerings to the fathers and mothers of nature) in the specific places that the Mother designated according to tradition.

ꞱE' CHWI

Ɉeri chow chwamʉ kawa ni; kuya'ba' pari izátikuma awnanʉngwasi.

Chwi zweykwey na'nonno, ʉyéy nanu nanʉn kínkiri emi ka'gumʉ tina anikátikumey zoriza ni.

Niwi ikʉ wíntukwa nʉnkureykase'ri ʉyéy a'bori zorie' pari. Iwákʉkin, sigin ey kínki, kʉn, ɉe', chwi azoya ni.

Niwi kʉzʉne'ri emi ɉe' chwi zweykwa siri tina imʉ na'nari, tikʉrigʉn ayeygwi i'ngwi nánukin chwi zwein umún inʉ ikwʉn nʉ'na niwikʉnisiza ni niwe'zʉnin, awiri ʉyéy kinki apaw ikwʉyekʉ ɉwi ekʉzusi, ingʉri rinʉnni'sa awiri niwikunsanʉ se' rékʉnʉn awʉn du na'nanno.

Umún kinki pinnase' ɉwi, zamʉ, zownʉ a'wekumʉn nugékʉri NAWOWA Nani, ɉiwʉ a'kwey zwein nuga, ʉyari pinna ɉe' zʉpáw nari zoya name' AWIKɄCHɄ kéywʉri ɉe' ipésʉyʉn, kʉn kʉta ayeygwi a'zasari wazoya ni, ɉecho' chwʉzʉnin ayeygwi. Ema ɉe kinki ʉazasari ukumʉngwa neykari SIMɄNɄ ꞱE'TERINKɄNA ɉe'zey kinki nari a'bunna name. Diwʉ́n nazey na' nari.

SAVE WATER

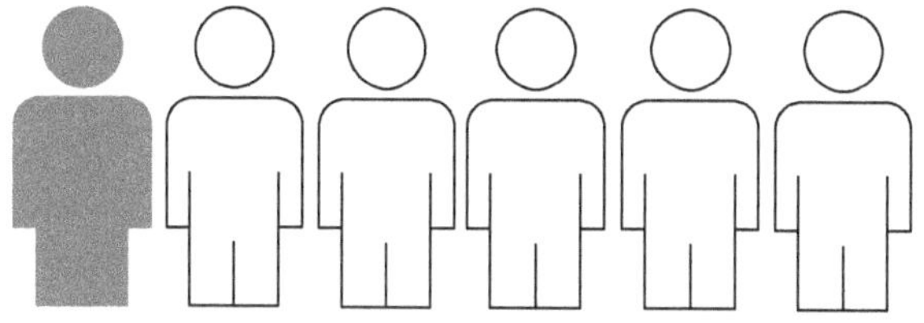

1 in 6 people
Do NOT have access to drinking water.

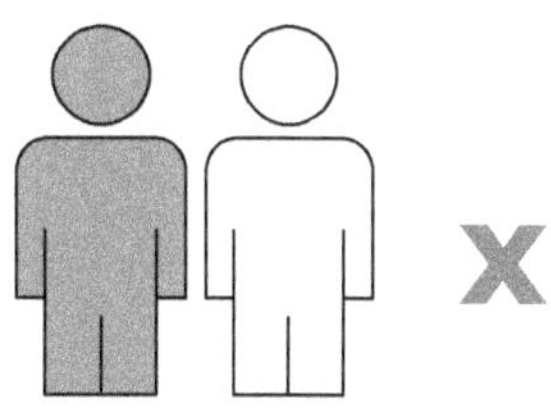

x

Water use has increased **more than 2 times** the rate of population increase.

A water faucet that drips once per second **wastes 27,000 gallons of water a year**.

Bath or Shower	Toilet	Laundry

17%	**27%**	**22%**

7.8. PEDAGOGICAL ACTIVITIES:

1. Research the history of JWIKUNOWMA with the Mamo in your community.

2. How can we take care of water at home?

3. What can we do to preserve water so we don't run out of it?

NIKAMɄ

1. Mamʉ mipowruse' zánʉsin ɈWIKɄNOWMA zʉkunsamʉ eygumʉn sisa awkwa.

2. Mikeynakʉri azi nisi ɉe áchwʉya no.

3. Azi nikamʉ niwikawʉnno ɉe neyka kʉchona aw nanʉngwasi.

IKʉN NUMBERS
AND OTHER LATIN AMERICAN INDIGENOUS MATH

8. ARHUACO NUMBERS
(Pronunciation in Iku language):

IZʉNCHʉNHAKUMʉYA IKʉN

1. (In'gwi)	11. (In'gwiuga in'gwikʉtoʉ) o ((1x10) + 1)
2. (Mowga)	12. (In'gwiuga mowgakʉtoʉ) o ((1x10) + 2)
3. (Máykʉnʉ)	13. (In'gwi uga máykʉnʉ kʉtow) o ((1x10) + 3)
4. (Ma´keywa)	14. (In'gwi uga ma´keywa kʉtow) o ((1x10) + 4)
5. (Asewa)	15. (In'gwi uga asewa kʉtow) o ((1x10) + 5)
6. (Chinwa)	16. (In'gwi uga chinwa kʉtow) o ((1x10) + 6)
7. (Koga)	17. (In'gwi uga koga kʉtow) o ((1x10) + 7)
8. (Abewa)	18. (In'gwi uga abewa kʉtow) o ((1x10) + 8)
9. (Ikawa)	19. (In'gwi uga ikawa kʉtow) o ((1x10) + 9)
10. (Uga)	20. (Mowga uga) o (2x10)

Currently composed by a decimal system, from zero (0) to nine (9); although, it is highly probable that the Iku did not have the concept of zero centuries ago. Thus, this could be an adaptation of western numerical systems.

Izʉnchʉnhakumʉya neykari cero awiri ikawakin neyka ní, ikʉ nʉnaba'ri cero ku' neyka nʉn nanki, ey andi ema neykari bunachʉ neykase' ayey re'gawi nʉnname' iwari emey kawi neyka ni.

It should be noted that interacting and teaching to native communities may require a different approach to those used in urban societies.

Emi in'geygwi neyka eygumʉn kumʉ a'nisi zakacho'samʉ kaweykari ema awí awkwa neyka awiri chuzanisi neyka ikʉ nʉnanke' kʉwasi awkweykari diwʉngwi kawi kʉwakamʉ kaw nanno bunachʉ winkwey zoya'ba kaway kaw nari.

Not all native tribes are equal, their languages, geographic locations and their willingness to accept outsiders will vary from one community to another.

Yow ikʉ ɉuna kwey ʉweykari ayey gunti neki na'nu neykani; winde'rimasʉya'ba, ka'gʉmʉse' wina'kwey zoya'ba awiri o'kʉrigʉn zanʉ neyka winipari zoya'ba.

Therefore, adaptation to each group will be essential for a successful implementation of numerical systems in their culture and daily life.

Ey awʉndi, in'gweti nʉnay ema a'zʉnchʉnhamʉ neykari emeykʉchʉ kawi ʉyasin siggin bunsi chari zoya'ba nʉka'mʉkanʉyʉn wina'zari neyka ni.

In the particular case of the Arhuacos, one of the ways to reach such an approach can be through the teaching of other numerical systems developed and widely used by other native communities, especially those Latin American civilizations that could be related to the Iku or be seen as Big Brothers to the Iku.

In'geygwi áykʉnʉ ikʉ arhuaku nʉnanke, ema neykasin mʉchey kʉnisi zeykweykari, in'geygwi ikʉ neykazey izʉnchʉnhakumʉya anʉkʉriwí zoya'ba ema re'masi akwey zweín nugeykazey ɉwa'sʉyame' atʉgekʉ winkwey zoyasin ʉnka'mʉkánʉkwey nigga ni.

8.1. WHICH AMERICAN INDIGENOUS TRIBES HAVE WE CONSIDERED?

BEMA IKɄ ɈUNA AMERICA WINKUYARI "ɄYA" AWANɄN NU'KURE?

Before beginning the presentation of the numerical systems of the selected tribes, it is important to recognize there are many other tribes throughout the continent that may have used other numerical systems, and that they all deserve further investigation and study.

Ema a'zʉnchʉnhamʉ ɉuna neyka ikʉ ingweti nʉnay eyki wasay kíngwiri, ayeygwi ema ka'gʉmʉ aɉu nʉna'bari in'geygwi ikʉ ɉuna neyka sʉmʉgwi winkwey zweín nugeykari izʉnchʉnhamʉ ɉuna neykari eygwi winʉkʉnanʉn nugga nanu nanno, ey andi sekʉnanamʉ awiri kʉriwiamʉgwi kaw nanno.

For this particular textbook, our research and analysis was limited to the numerical systems used by the main tribes that reigned in large areas of present-day Peru and Mesoamerica, an area that extends approximately from central Mexico, through Belize, Guatemala, El Salvador, Honduras, Nicaragua and northern Costa Rica.

Emazey paperi kʉrigawínkʉnari, sekanari awiri ka'zarunhakumey uneykari gugingwi izʉnchʉnhamʉ ɉuna neykasin in'geygwi ikʉ iwa Perú winkwʉn nugeykase' awiri Mesoamérica, ka'gʉmʉ in'gwi aɉu awʉtari zari México sí pari, Belice ʉnkʉzagi, Guatemala, El Salvador, Honduras, Nikaragua awiri Costa Rica zwʉrakiargʉnkin wina'kwey nʉneykase' winʉkʉnari neykagwi nanu nanno.

In that vast geographical area, the pre-Columbian civilizations of the Incas, Aztecs and Maya flourished until their annihilation during the Spanish conquest in the fifteenth and sixteenth centuries (1400-1600).

Eymanke' ka'gʉmʉ awʉtari zari nʉna'ba, Incas, Azteca, awiri Maya eygumʉn awʉtari inʉ chuzʉnhasi rizweín nu'nari sémʉke bunachʉ España zanʉ neykase' winde'riɉo'si siglo XV awiri XVI (1400-1600) ey awkin chʉká a'zʉnnari, yow izátikumʉkin.

The brutality of the conquest along with some inter-tribal wars fragmented these great civilizations, leaving only scattered descendants with little cultural connection with their ancestors.

Ema ka'gʉmʉ ke awari zoya gugin arunhu nari ey awi keywʉri agʉnke' a'kwey rizoya ɉinari ʉnwinʉnkʉripanʉn pana ʉweykasindi ema ɉinari yow winʉkʉrichona una ní, in'gwí atʉgʉnkekʉ winkwey zoya ɉina zʉn chúkumey. Emey ʉwe'ki, izʉnchʉnhakumʉya neykari eyki

However, the advanced numerical systems of these societies have survived and could offer practical benefits to native tribes that still in existence today, for example, by creating a cultural link between the Iku and other existing native communities, as well as with their predecessors.

iwákʉkin kwey chʉká a'zari nanʉn nugga nanu nanno in'geygwi eykigwi ikʉ ɉuna izátikuma awkingwi neykase', ewe'ri ikʉ neykase' awiri in'geygwi neykase', kunsamʉ nari ʉnwinkikwasa awaki nugga ní.

8.2. HOW ADVANCED WERE THEIR MATH METHODS? AND HOW ARE THEY RELEVANT TODAY?

¿BIN NÁNʉKIN IZʉNCHʉNHAKUMʉYARI ÁZWʉRÁRIGʉN NʉN NANNO? AWIRI, ¿IWARI AZI KAWI EYGUMʉN ZAKACHO'KUMO?

The Incas, Aztecs and Mayas used their mathematical skills in astronomy, as in other daily activities, such as construction, agriculture, commerce or exchange of goods, and much more.

Incas, kwa Azteca awiri Maya nenanki a'zʉnchʉnhakumʉyeykari chʉkimʉrwakʉ wirako'ku ɉina chuzari awʉn nugga'ba' a'mʉkʉnhasi zoyana ní, awiri siggin emi bunsi ichari inʉ ʉnkawi zoya'ba, urakʉ ʉngʉwin, ʉnzarikʉyʉn, inʉ ʉnkʉngeykʉyʉn kwa ʉnkʉnta'sʉyʉn, awiri eygumʉn na'ba neki.

It is recommended that the study of the numerical system be carried out according to its level of complexity and the abilities of the students.

Ema inʉ izʉnchʉnhamʉ neyka ʉnkʉriwí awizʉneyka ikʉse'ri, ikʉnha winʉkʉnʉnʉ'kin awiri ema winde'riwí ʉweykase' kʉnikʉyʉkin zʉn winɉwa'samʉ kawa ní.

A simple way to start could be with the Incas, then the Aztecs and finally, with the Maya. This order also reflects the systems and applications closest to how the numerical systems are currently used in most countries.

Ema neyka nánʉkin re'gawi ne ʉnkwasaykwa nanʉndi, Inca neykasin keywʉ nanu nanno, ey unáyuri Azteca awiri, akowna nékʉri Maya. Ema re'nisi nʉnaygwi kawi chuzʉnhasʉyari emi pinna ɉuna inʉ kwey a'bori zoya'bagwi in'gwi mi'na ba'ba úkumey nakʉn nugga ní.

It should be noted that these mathematical skills should be relevant today, and their application in more advanced systems, such as applied science, technology, engineering and mathematics, and could be of great value for future generations. Especially when solving technological, environmental, humanistic and others similar challenges.

Finally, these numerical systems can serve existing native communities, and provide access to additional mathematical and scientific skills, without being perceived as an authoritative interference by Western cultures, but rather, as a continuation and adoption of previous native cultures.

Emey awari izeywámʉsʉkwa nanʉndi izʉnchʉnhakumʉyari iwari eygumʉn kinki be neki a'mʉkʉnhakumey zweinó, máquina ɉina nʉna'ba, inʉ wasi ukumʉya'ba, ɉwisía ʉnkʉzagichʉn nuga'ba, gunti awʉtari chuzari nanʉn nugga nanu nanno, ema neykari eygwi nakʉngweykase'ri ɉwisía ɉina nʉna'ba, kʉn ɉuna nʉna'ba, arunhey chʉká kʉzari nanʉn nuga'ba gunti emasindi kʉre'guka una nikʉngwa nanu nanno.

Akowna nékʉri, ema kingwi neykari ikʉ ɉina azey azey winkwey neykase'ri, eygwi diwʉn nari neki winʉka'mʉkanʉkweygwi nari nanʉngwa nanu nanno, ʉya ɉweɉwe nari kinki nanu nari, emi iwa winkwey zweín nuga'ba ayey nisi aya'ba anipʉnsi gunti atʉgʉnkérigʉn zanʉ kwasʉn nukaygwi nari.

8.3. WHEN AND WHERE DID THEY EXIST?

¿BINZARI AWIRI BEKɄ WINKWANANNO?

Incas (Peru, South America)
1400s - 1572
Estimated Population: 10 million
Peak of its Civilization: 1430s

Azteca (Mesoamerica)
1100 - 1600s
Estimated Population: 7 million
Peak of its Civilization: 1500s

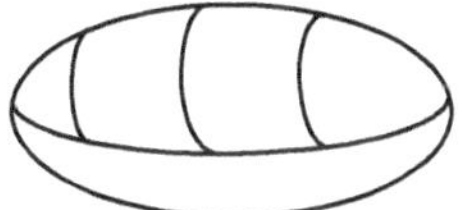

Maya (Mesoamerica)
1800 BC - 1687
Estimated Population: 7 million
Peak of its Civilization: 200-400

8.4. THE MATHEMATICS OF THE MAYA AND AZTECS: ABACO MAYA OR NEPOHUALTZINTZIN

IZʉCHʉNKWEYNA MAYA AWIRI AZTECAZEY: ABACO MAYA

(Ne-Pohuali-Tzintzin) means having similar small items counted by one person

Both the Aztecs and the Maya used similar calculation tools based on the vigesimal system (base 20), although with slightly different applications in their calendars.

Azteca awiri Maya ɟinari inʉ izʉnchʉnhey awizari kʉwasi awkwey neyka kʉnari nʉnnaní, mowga uga tekʉre'pʉnkwa (vigesimal base 20), timasin inʉ kʉwasi timasin uneykari diwʉn kawi kʉnʉnnanki.

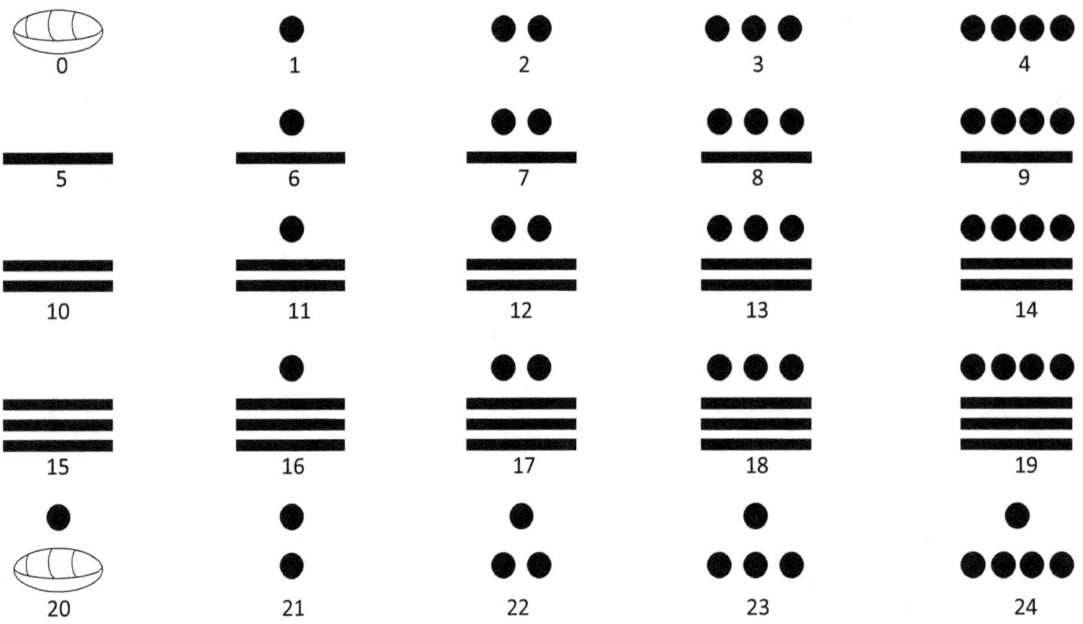

The Maya abacus or Nepohualtzintzin consists of a grid made with rods and seeds that represented the numbers.

Abaco Maya neykari re'sasá kawi wariyasin bunna awiri ayaba'ri zaɟunari iazʉnchʉnhakumʉya kʉzʉna nʉnna ni.

In the lower part there are four counts, which in the first row have unit values (or 1, 2, 3 and 4), and in the upper part there are three accounts, with values

Ʉndérigʉndi ma'keywa re'nikwa nari nʉnnani, ayaba'ri (0,1,2,3,4) iwa azwʉrakiari maykʉnʉ izʉnchʉnha neyka (5,10,15)

of five units (or 5, 10 and 15), respectively.

The counts in the additional columns have values assigned depending on the numerical system in base 20.

For the Mayans and the Aztecs, counting at base 20 was completely natural, since the use of sandals allowed them to use their toes, as well as the fingers of their hands, to count and do calculations.

emey kawi izʉnchʉnhakumʉya winʉkʉnʉnna ni.

A’zʉnchʉnhakumʉya neykari mowga uga neyka ʉnpʉnsi zoya ey awga ni.

Maya awiri Aztekase’ri mowga uga neykari ayey kawi winʉkʉnʉna zʉn neyka ni, sʉpatu re’yusi winzoya’ba asewa kʉttʉ zʉwa kʉnari zoya’ba awiri guna’ asewagwi neykasin zʉn izʉnchʉnhey nʉnna ni.

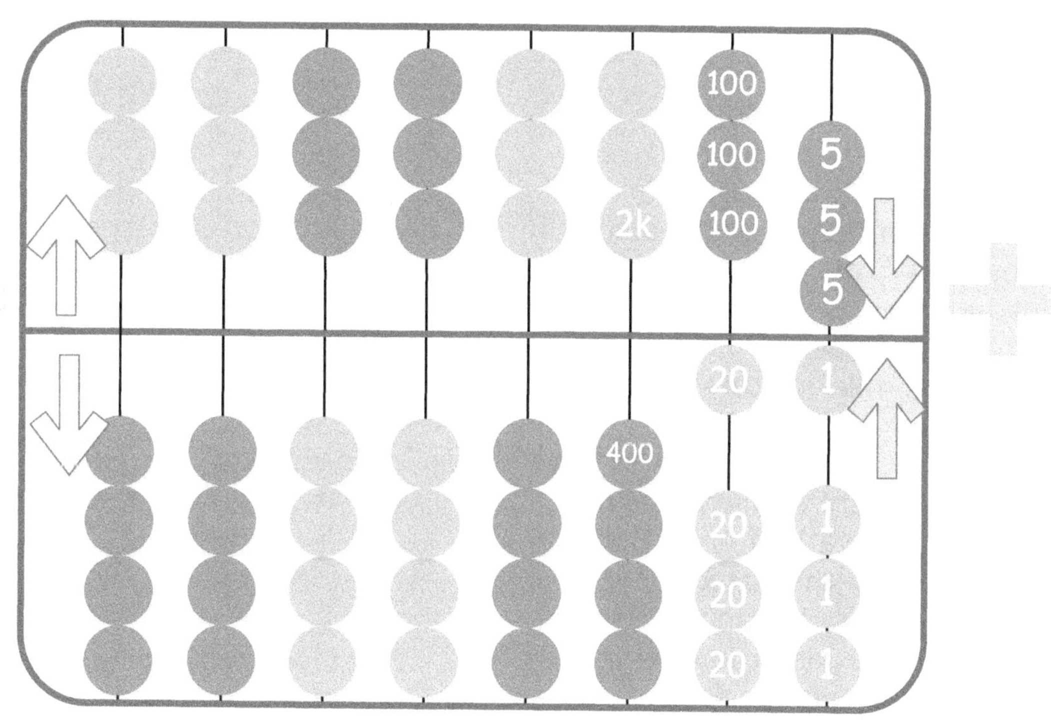

20 + (15 + 1) = 36

A complete Mayan abacus would have 13 rows with 7 accounts in each row, representing 91 accounts in each Nepohualtzintzin. This number, 91, is a basic number to understand the close relationship

Abaco Mayazeyri in’gwi uga maykʉnʉ kʉttow re’sanuka kʉnariri koga izʉnchʉnha re’sanukʉya kʉnari gunti ikawa uga in’gwi kʉttow Nepohualtzintzin kʉnʉnna ni. Ey awʉndi ema ikawa uga in’gwi

between the Maya and certain natural phenomena that they observed.

kʉttow neykari akʉttʉ winʉkʉnʉnna ni, eymasin emi ka'gʉmʉse' zari zoyeykari winchwʉn un'na ni.

For example:

1 Nepohualtzintzin (91) = Number of days on each season of the year
2 Nepohualtzintzin (182) = Number of days of the corn cycle
3 Nepohualtzintzin (273) = Number of days of gestation of a baby
4 Nepohualtzintzin (364) = 1 Complete cycle and approximately one year

It is worth noting that both huge spatial quantities and infinitesimal small quantities can be calculated with absolute precision in the Maya Abacus.

Ema Maya inʉ a'zʉnchʉnkweyna winʉkʉnari uneykari warekʉ zari zari awʉngweykari ayey nikʉngwʉkin ka'chori zoyana ni.

There have been also very ancient abacus attributed to the Olmec culture, and some bracelets of Mayan origin also known as Maya Calculators. Furthermore, a variety of other forms and materials have been found in similar cultures.

Emey gunti nari eygwi eygumʉn inʉ winde'ritasi ki zoyananno awanʉkwey nari pinnakʉchʉ kʉnariki zoya nanno awanʉkwey nari kawi chuzʉna ni, calvuladora awga neki diwʉn kawi nʉnkwe'ki eygwi kʉnʉnna ni.

Astronomy is perhaps one of the most important applications of these numerical systems. Both the Maya and the Aztecs developed very advanced calendars in which they managed to make very detailed and precise measurements of our planet and its relationship with other elements in space, such as the sun and the moon, as well as Earth's relationship with other planets and stars.

Eymi awanʉkwa nanʉndi Maya awiri Azteca neykari ema azʉnchʉnhey awkweykari emi wirako'ku ɉina chʉkimʉrwakʉ chuzari nanʉn nugga neykasindi ema tima ʉnta'kumey zoya eygumʉn kʉra' winɉwa'si ʉyari ɉwia'sin kʉzagichi zoyari yow re'gu'na winʉkʉnari nanʉn un'na ni.

Emeygwi nari inʉ wasi awkweyka gwakʉn akingwi.

Another important element of the Mayan calendar is the concept known as Long Count or initial

In'geygwi neykari ema izʉnchʉnhey awkweykasindi pinna yown re'gu'na gun nare'ri

series, which allowed the Maya to count long periods of time, such as tens, hundreds or thousands of years. Such advanced system estimated o established a day zero (0) as the beginning of the Mayan calendar, that day was estimated by the Maya as August 11 of the year 3,114 BC.

The dates were noted in a special way using points to separate the days, months and years. Which, together with other advanced concepts in their calendars, facilitates mathematical manipulation in a simple and standardized way.

In the textbook,
Native Mathematics 5-6,
ISBN: 978-0-9997757-1-4, you can find more details about this and other concepts related to native mathematics, its applications in astronomy, science and nature.

inʉ izʉnchʉnhey awkweykari sʉmʉ a'zʉnchʉnkwey neykagwi kʉnanu nʉnnanno, kʉggi'sin ɉwiasin kʉzagichi zoyeyka ayey kawi anʉkʉnʉnna ni. Emey ʉwame' tma agosto 11 zare'ri 3.114 Cristo kwakumu'gwiri, eymi keywʉ kʉggi'ri ʉnpesi zweingwa re'gowna ni.

Emey nare'ri ɉwía , tima kwa kʉggi neykari puntu gawi kwa eyna isi zʉn wina'zʉchʉnhana ni, emey nari gunti unʉkiri nánʉkin nanay gunti kawi atʉgʉnkékʉkin ʉntamena ʉwa nanu nanno.

Ema paperi kʉriwiwkweyna,
Native Mathematics 5-6,
ISBN: 978-0-9997757-1-4,
neykase'ri eygumʉn kʉriwin me'ɉunʉn kinkiri eygumʉn ey ku'nanno, pinna ka'gʉmʉse' inʉ kwey chuzari na'ba tá warunhʉn kinkiri awiri bemʉke' a'mʉkʉnhasʉn me'ɉunʉn kinkiri.

Baktun
20 Katunes
144,000 Days

Katun
20 Tunes
7,200 Days

Tun
18 Uninales
360 Days

Uninal
20 Kines
20 Days

Kin
1 Day

The Authors...

M.Eng. Ernesto Vega Jánica
Electrical Engineer and Master in Fire Protection Engineering with 20 years of experience. Member of IEEE, NFPA and SFPE. Recognized as the Engineer of the Year in 2017 by the New Jersey Chapter of the Society of Fire Protection Engineers (SFPE) and honored with the Tyco Patent Award in 2011. Instructor of international standards and author of multiple publications worldwide.

PhD. Simón Esmeral Ariza
Associate researcher of Colciencias, Doctorate in Education, Ex-Secretary of Education, Head of Technical Activities, Principal and Director of the Regional Unit of Ethno-Education with more than 30 years of experience in the service of teaching to indigenous communities. University professor with countless publications and recognitions in the educational, multicultural and ethical field.

Lic. Hugues Vega Murgas
Bachelor's Degree in Social Sciences, Journalist and Author of multiple educational textbooks. Mr. Vega Murgas has extensive experience at the executive level of Secretary of Education for more than 30 years. Former Director of literacy plans, educational universalization plans and Chief Technical Director. In addition to serving as a university professor for more than 10 years, he has led multiple ethno-educational initiatives in several Departments of the Colombian Caribbean Region.

Special Acknowledge...

Nelson García Torres
Linguist Advisor Iku/Arhuaco

We thank all those people with whom we have had the pleasure of working during this project. Especially to our families, whose love and guidance are with us every step of the way.

We would like to thank the Arhuaco tribe, natives of the Sierra Nevada de Santa Marta, Colombia, for their wisdom and guidance during the development of these activities.

We are also tankful to the reviewers, linguists and other experts for their assistance, peer reviewing and comments that greatly improved the initial manuscript, although we recognize that any mistakes are ours and should not tarnish the reputation of these esteemed people.

Duní gunti rekeykumuyun ema nikamu re'wekumey zoyana'ba niwikuchwi uneyka jina. Eygumun kinki ayeygwi zeyzey rekukumuyeykari niwisinamu ni, zeyzeygwi niwiwari emi niwi ingiti untameri zorikuray ánugwe niwikusana. Zeynari reni.

Arwaku tana neyka gwakun duní gunti rekeykumuyun, a zunhumunuse' winkwey zwein nugga; kunsamu winugunsi zweín nugga neykasin íngunu niwekugasi zoyaname' ema nikamu neykazey nari.

Ema nikamu sekununna, ga'kunamu jwa'suya awiri uyazey jwa'suya neyka gwakun akingwi duní gunti keykumuyun emiri emey kawin gunti awari du niwekukusi uneyka gwakun akingwi, nanamuri kwa iba'ri du kaw nunnige'ri niwigwi niwikawungwa nanunanno awiri emey uwame' buni'gumu nariza neki nanu nariza nanu nanno.emey gun ti awgin. Duní.

www.ingramcontent.com/pod-product-compliance
Lightning Source LLC
LaVergne TN
LVHW081403110826
845149LV00010B/1651

* 9 7 8 0 9 9 9 7 7 5 7 3 8 *